Buen Camino and Bon Appétit

A Culinary Journey and Pilgrimage
with Ingredients

Eduard Peyer

All rights reserved. No part of this book shall be reproduced or transmitted in any form or by any means, electronic, mechanical, magnetic, photographic including photocopying, recording or by any information storage and retrieval system, without prior written permission of the publisher. No patent liability is assumed with respect to the use of the information contained herein. Although every precaution has been taken in the preparation of this book, the publisher and author assume no responsibility for errors or omissions. Neither is any liability assumed for damages resulting from the use of the information contained herein.

Copyright © 2012 by Eduard Peyer

ISBN 978-0-7414-7869-6 Black and White Paperback
ISBN 978-0-7414-7827-6 Color Paperback
ISBN 978-0-7414-7922-8 Color Hardcover
ISBN 978-0-7414-7828-3 eBook
Library of Congress Control Number: 2012944521

Printed in the United States of America

Published August 2012

INFINITY PUBLISHING
1094 New DeHaven Street, Suite 100
West Conshohocken, PA 19428-2713
Toll-free (877) BUY BOOK
Local Phone (610) 941-9999
Fax (610) 941-9959
Info@buybooksontheweb.com
www.buybooksontheweb.com

Contents

Foreword	*1*
Introduction	*7*
1. Walking the Way of Saint James	*11*
2. My Culinary Education and Apprenticeship	*37*
3. A Young Chef in Switzerland	*57*
4. Putting Down Roots in the United States	*107*
5. A Growing Family, a Flourishing Career	*123*
Postscript	*147*
Recipes	*155*

Foreword

Pilgrimage as Moveable Feast

One consequence of studying mythology, both collective and personal, is the overriding conviction that, as the mythologist Joseph Campbell often affirmed, we are each called to a specific destiny. Regarding the individual, Campbell claimed, having studied world mythologies for most of his professional life, the first obligation to destiny is that one must hear the call, the vocation, the voice to which one is destined. Indeed, some never hear it. But if one does, then one is confronted with a choice: to heed the call or to postpone it or even refuse it. No calls collect; one must choose. Many select one of the last two options and live their lives alienated from what they were beckoned to achieve. If one decides to heed the call, then one gives one's self over to something beyond him or herself and enters the woods of one's destiny. It is a complex interplay of free choice and fatedness working together.

Now in entering the woods one must be sure that: 1. it is thickest where one enters, not the easiest or least brambled or thinnest aperture. Further, one must be sure that there is not a path already trodden, for if so, then one risks following the calling of another, not one's own and so lives a counterfeit life in the footsteps of a destiny already assigned to another. Finally, and at least initially, one must go it alone, not with a group or a tribe or a village surrounding one, for then one never settles into the full consciousness such a journey, and here I will choose the term pilgrimage, requires. *Buen Camino & Bon Appétit* is just such a pilgrimage that Eddie Peyer relays to us through three interwoven stories.

The first story which opens the pilgrimage relates his experience in June and July, 2011, when, with his daughter Francesca and his daughter-in-law, Valerie, he was led to the Camino de Santiago in the French Pyrenees to walk the 500 miles to the majestic cathedral of Santiago—Saint James—in Santiago de Compostela, a word that conjures both "field of stars" and compost, or cemetery, a locale where the fiery stars of life reflect their white light on the earthy loam of death. That is journey #1. Journey #2 is his pilgrimage back in time to his youth in Lucerne, Switzerland in his teens where he heard, then heeded, the call. One day, as he related to me over lunch, when he was working for a cleaning company, he found himself on a ladder in a kitchen of a fine restaurant washing the air ducts that emanated from the ceiling. While he was cleaning, he looked down at the pots and pans, the dishes being prepared, the bustle of the chefs and assistants and the thought struck him: "this could be an interesting place to work."

Listening to him relate this story, I suggested that he pilgrimaged to this calling from the heights of a ladder looking down into the landscape of the kitchen; in that moment he voyaged from cleaning dirty ducts to glazing and roasting ducks, a comparison he enjoyed. From ducts to ducks is the manner in which the soul moves, interrogates, discovers and rests, finally on what we have today reduced to calling a career. But it is much more than that mythically: it is a calling; one is called to a task and to a life that fulfills part of the purpose of the cosmos. When he climbed down from that ladder, Eddie had seen the burning bush and a voice that called him to a life of meaning.

The third journey is one into the complex, delicious and wondrously creative world of food itself and the alchemy of its preparation, which is both an art and science at once. The preparation of food is one of the oldest human activities, stretching back into prehistory, so Eddie had more than a few ancestors he was following, but in his own culinary style.

Each food has its own story, each ingredient its own narrative and every condiment its own plot structure. Put them together and one has a recipe of complexity that one can flavor to taste. Few narratives possess the nuance, the instinct, the flavor of food preparation itself. Eddie was drawn early on to the serenity of sauces, to the marvelous seasoning flavors that sauces can improve what it endorses. Some delicious gradations attend the creating of sauces and this final condiment can make or break a fine dish. I think that there is an inner poetic in sauces; it is what flavors our lives if done correctly, warmed just right, served at just the right time and poured over life's more massive foods to give flavor, if not pure joy, in the tasting. We even speak of saucy people, the sauce of life, the ingredient of the imagination that makes the commonplace transform into something magical. These are the three pilgrimages that *Buen Camino* serves up to us in three main dishes, all served to be savored at once, chewed slowly, so one can relish how each contributed to a moveable feast of a life lived well.

Following on the tradition of the ancient art of pilgrimage, and of the Camino, one of the oldest and fast-becoming the most popular path for today's pilgrims (see www.americanpilgrims.com), this path called to Eddie to traverse. That he accomplished it with his two beautiful female companions adds piquancy to the journey. But this move onto the ancient footpath when in his late 60s also provoked another journey, as I have suggested, back, into his biography, to the roots of his coming-into-consciousness at age 16 when he was called to his path as a chef, which earned him renown in both Europe and the United States and from which he recently retired.

In turning to memory as a vocational path, Eddie was compelled by an inner voice to set the stories down, make the road a bit more discernible, to remember the countless vignettes of his early days as a cook, the grueling schedules that often left one time to sleep only a few hours each night, of being given the responsibility early on at a first class hotel to prepare and serve Dinner each day to 45 very discerning chefs, knowing full well he would be judged by such an august body and his reputation enhanced or dismantled. The stories themselves, coming one after another in rapid succession, are in fact the ingredients of the casserole of his life, a mix of flavors that will only be simmered once in the history of the world, Eddie wished to set it down right. And this task he has achieved admirably, as anyone who reads his story will affirm.

Towards the end of his narrative, Eddie introduces, with mouth-watering photos, which he took himself, of the dishes he recreated in his home in Texas, dishes that played major roles in his pilgrimage through life: his development as a first class head chef; his migration to America, and his walk on the Camino. Each recipe begins with a short description of the situation he was in that brought the aromas of just that fish, meat, flan, soup, or stew forward in his life. The foods he ate are as much an organic part of his past, present and future, as anything he has written. Recipes carry their own rhetoric, their own grammar, their own unique parts of speech and persuasive appeal. Put a recipe's parts all in the right order and measure, and what grows from it is so much grander than the sum of its parts. Recipes are alchemical blueprints to the elixirs, the grails of good dining, one of the greatest gifts of human beings to one another. Bon appetite indeed!

Savor the stories, try a recipe or two, and remember in your own life when a particular meal, a unique dish, an exceptional combination of wine with a favorite fare changed you, made you more human, increased your appetite for life in all its variegated vegetable vastness. Who would outlaw a grand meal with those you love, to be labeled a pilgrimage to the soul of hospitality itself? Therein resides the power of Eddie's story, so take it in one modest bite at a time, chew it slowly and allow it to digest under its own terms. You will leave the table full of stories that add further spices to your life. What can compete with vibrant narratives unfolding under the clatter of a delicious repast? The stories are a form of the Camino and the banquet itself—well--enjoy!

Dennis Patrick Slattery, Ph.D.
Author of *Grace in the Desert:*
Awakening to the Gifts of Monastic Life
New Braunfels, Texas
8 July 2012.

Introduction

In the spring of 2011, I walked the Camino de Santiago with my daughter Francesca and my daughter-in-law Valerie. Pilgrimages to Santiago have not ceased since medieval times, when St. James's remains were allegedly discovered in Galicia. Some 260 trails, starting as far away as Russia and Poland, wind their ways through Europe, all ending at the impressive Cathedral of Santiago de Compostela. We traveled 800 kilometers on foot in forty days on the best-known and most popular route, the Camino Francès, starting at the foot of the Pyrenees in Saint-Jean-Pied-de-Port, France, and ending in the city of Santiago de Compostela. Our journey was a spiritual pilgrimage dedicated to the mother of my children, who had been taken away from us way too early in life. It was the second big journey I had completed in six months. The first, my journey as a professional chef, had lasted almost half a century. Business and work had always been the priorities. That journey had ended late in 2010.

This second journey, my pilgrimage along the Camino de Santiago, brought back vivid memories of my life as a young chef in Switzerland. Never before had I had that much time to reflect on my life. It also brought back memories of many of the dishes I had prepared during those years. Somehow the food and the memories were all intertwined, which is not surprising, since my passion for great food has shaped my professional life.

This book is a record of both of those journeys. It is the story of how I developed as a chef and as a person. It is, in a sense, a photo album of my life, except that the snapshots are the dishes I prepared and the memories they evoke. At the end of the book are some of those "snapshots." I hope that you will enjoy them as much as I did.

As Francesca, Valerie, and I left the city of Santiago in northwestern Spain by train and rolled over the tracks toward the Madrid Chamartín railway station on our journey home, I thought back on my recent experiences. The stress of traveling 800 kilometers on foot, a short illness, and a dangerous fall in the steep hills above Molinaseca were all behind me now. The three of us enjoyed the comfort of the reclining seats as we looked out the window at the lush Spanish countryside. I began to think about the thoughts and memories that had flooded over me during my pilgrimage.

My mind drifted back into the past, half a century ago, to the time when I started my culinary career as a 16-year-old kid in an old hotel in Engelberg, Switzerland. I also was thinking of my escape over the mountains to nowhere, a journey that frightened my employer, my co-workers, and all of my family. I thought of the outstanding chefs and mentors I have had the opportunity to learn from and reminisced about the harsh conditions and long hours we had to endure. I thought of the many friends and colleagues I had worked with through summer and winter seasons in luxury resort kitchens in Europe. These were good times, despite the fact that we were screamed at every day and worked months without a day off. I thought about Henry Jolidon, our instructor at culinary school in Lake Zug in Switzerland, and the cognac-infused cigars he savored and about listening to the many fascinating stories he told as we sat around a fireplace during freezing November nights. I was thinking of my mentor, Chef Rüegsegger, who had entrusted me with handling special private dinners for Sophia Loren and numerous other celebrities at the Bürgenstock golf club. I remembered the days in Davos during the World Figure Skating Championships in January of 1966, when a physician visited our kitchens when we were all near exhaustion to give us booster shots to keep us going for another day. My mind drifted back even farther, to when I still lived at home. I thought of my father, who had so much patience with me when I was a young and rebellious teenager. I had no interest working for my father's small iron construction and locksmith business. But he was always there for me and supported me. I had no clue about what I wanted to do after I was thrown out of prep school at the Institute Sainte-Marie in Martigny. I must have been a bit too much to handle for the Catholic monks, too rebellious. I was much more focused on playing with the soccer team than on religious teachings.

The first high-rise buildings of Madrid brought me back to the present. One more night in a suburban apartment hotel near Madrid-Barajas Airport, and then the next day we would be home in Texas. One of my journeys would come to an end. Or was it really a beginning? Perhaps walking the Camino has become a new passion for me.

1. Walking the Way of Saint James

As I completed the tenth stage of my journey along the Camino de Santiago, I checked into the municipal *albergue* (hostel) in Azofra. I was exhausted in the 95-degree heat, and I took off my boots and socks and soaked my feet in the small and shallow cold water pool in the hostel's courtyard. I was aware that I had pushed myself a bit too hard that day, as perhaps I had during some of the earlier stages, for example when I began the pilgrimage in Saint-Jean-Pied-de-Port at the foot of the French Pyrenees. Some of my companions had repeatedly told me that my pace was too fast. Now with 165 kilometers behind us, my body began to remind me that I did need a rest. Could it be the two or maybe three too many glasses of Albariño I had drunk the night before with Marianne and Connie under the shady cherry tree in Ventosa? Or perhaps it was the thought of the pasta dinner with wild mushrooms I had promised to prepare for all our pilgrim friends in Azofra that evening that tired me. We had bought the groceries as we passed through the city of Najera and schlepped them for six kilometers to the *albergue*. Tired as I was, I kept my word and prepared the supper, inviting everyone at the *albergue* to help themselves to fresh salads and penne pasta. After that, although I was exhausted, I still could not sleep for half the night.

I was thinking about our arrival in Logroño only two short nights ago and the 100 miles of trail we had completed since then. We felt rightly proud and physically fit. It was the longest walk we had ever done in our lives, although we knew that there were still 400 miles in front of us. Francesca and Valerie were happy to spend the night in a plush hotel instead of in a bunk bed in a hostel. The Gallego food festival at the Plaza Mayor that Sunday night reminded me of a typical Texas barbecue with the exception of the ever-present *pulpo gallego* (Galician octopus). The pimientos de Padrón tasted sensational, especially with a chilled mug of San Miguel Beer.

I was not in such great shape the following morning as I climbed out of my bunk bed at the *albergue* in Azofra; I immediately knew that something was terribly wrong with my balance. I had to hold on to the wall and the bed frame to stay on my feet. The whole world was spinning. I tried to stand for a few minutes and regained some of my equilibrium. After a cup of coffee, I tied my hiking boots, fastened my backpack, grabbed my pilgrim's cane, and hit the trail for the 23-kilometer stage to Grañon with a lunch break in Santo Domingo de la Calzada. Once more, I pushed it. I was walking with my friend Neil, and things went well until we reached Grañon. San Juan Bautista, our *albergue* for the night, was located two floors up in the church towers. As I attempted to climb the sparely lit staircase to our sleeping quarters, the dizziness and spinning returned, and I realized that sooner rather than later I would have to see a physician. We entered a large hall, where gym mats served as our beds. I grabbed two mats for extra cushioning and a blanket and lay down, hoping my dizziness would cease. Each time I opened my eyes, I was overcome with nausea, and the spinning was unbearable.

Francesca and Valerie had a few problems of their own, including blisters, bruised toenails, and signs of tendonitis. Despite these typical injuries, both *peregrinas* continued on the next stage to Belorado the following morning. I had to stay behind and seek help from a doctor, if one could be found. For the first time during the journey, scary thoughts crossed my mind: What could this be? I hadn't come this far to quit now. Wrapped in a blanket and still lying on the gym mats, I listened with my eyes closed to the sound of conversations in a half-dozen languages as everyone got busy that morning in preparation for another day of walking. Finally the gym was empty. I felt completely out of place lying there all alone, uncertain of what would happen next. I managed to climb one floor up, take a long shower, and get dressed. Flavia, one of the *hospitaleras*, a native of Brazil, sat me down near the window in the hostel's small dining area. By that time, all the pilgrims had left for the day. The friendly *hospitalera* handed me a cup of fresh coffee and began to massage my shoulders and neck, telling me she had been a practicing physician for many years in underdeveloped African countries. "I do not have a license to practice here in Spain," she said. "Now I dedicate my time to pilgrims like you." She thought I might have injured a vertebra from carrying the backpack, and that increased my concerns even more.

As the church bells rang at noon, we received word that a physician was scheduled to visit Grañon that day. That was good news, since the small village had no full-time doctor. Both Flavia and Franca, the other *hospitalera*, accompanied me to the doctor's office. We were laughing as I held on to the women and the women held on to me. The villagers probably thought, "Here's another drunken *peregrino*." I found myself sitting in a small waiting area in an old house at the end of the village together with a few local seniors, all of them holding on to their canes, patiently awaiting the traveling physician. I felt just like them, holding on to my own pilgrim cane. Luckily, I received the *peregrino* treatment and was seen right away when the young female physician arrived. By 1:30 that afternoon I was on my way again to Belorado, with a prescription of pills for my vertigo and a warning to walk at a slower pace. Why couldn't I practice what I preached? It was me who had repeatedly said: "You cannot manage the Camino, the Camino manages you." The prescription cost me three Euros and the visit was free, since I had no valid health card for Spain. Any other form of payment I had tried to offer was politely declined. "Buen Camino," the lady doctor had said.

Feeling drowsy but thankful to be able to continue the pilgrimage, I was on the trail again. Five hours later, I was happy to be reunited with my two companions and our Canadian friend Neil at the *albergue* Caminante in Belorado. We sat down for paella and a bottle of wine. The lady chef at the *albergue* really knew how to prepare Spain's national dish! It was delicious and perfectly done.

While you are walking the Camino de Santiago, eating dinner becomes a kind of a ritual. You know that you deserve that bottle of wine and the simple three-course meal, always fresh and simply prepared that huge basket of fresh bread to help you reload your carbohydrates. It is a special feeling of thankfulness: another day of walking is completed, another stage is behind you. That evening in Belorado, all of us had an ailment of some kind. Valerie had a badly bruised toenail, Francesca had developed full-blown tendonitis, Neil was limping badly with a sore knee, and I had vertigo and was taking prescription medicine! Four crippled *peregrines*, I thought. That night, as we were finishing our dinner, we evaluated our physical well-being and condition. The decision was unanimous; we would omit the next 38 kilometers of walking. The next morning, the four of us traveled by bus from Belorado to the city of Burgos.

Although I had been retired for five months, I still needed to learn how to slow down and enjoy life after leaving a stressful job in a highly demanding industry. The Way of St. James, a months'-long walking tour that ends in the city of Santiago de Compostela in Spain, presented me with a great opportunity to just do that. The time you are afforded to reflect and think about yourself seems endless as you walk this magnificent and historic trail. Francesca and I had dedicated this pilgrimage to Patricia, my late wife and the mother of our three children, who are now grown. She was a devout Catholic. We knew that she would have been with us on this journey if she had been alive.

Before this journey, we didn't know anything about the Camino de Santiago; I didn't even know that the trail crosses my home country from Lake Constance to Geneva. One of its stages even winds through my hometown of Lucerne, then continues to Geneva and from there through France and finally enters Spain, ending in Santiago de Compostela. The name "Via Jacobi" had popped up several times as I browsed through websites at home, looking for interesting hiking trails in Switzerland, and that is how I discovered the Camino de Santiago. Our fascination with it increased every day. We researched everything there is to know about it, on forums, blogs, and websites. Within a very short time we had decided to travel to Europe and walk "The Camino."

That summer in Spain, we met a number of people from different parts of the world—Germans, French, Irish, Japanese, Koreans, Hungarians, Dutch, Italians, Brazilians, Spaniards, and Portuguese. All of them had their own reasons for undertaking the journey. Four lovely Irish ladies from Dublin had walked The Way from Logroño in northern Spain to Santiago de Compostela in 2010, during the Holy Year, and had returned to complete the journey, walking from Saint-Jean-Pied-de-Port, France, to Logroño. I realized that they were true believers when they asked me to give the bronze statue of St. James a very special hug when I reached the cathedral in Santiago. Daniel from Seoul desperately needed a break from his daily routine and had traveled all the way to Spain. Karen, a newlywed Canadian who was soon to start a new career in Atlanta, had decided to walk 100 miles on the Camino before returning to the United States. Randy, an Irishman from Dublin, like most of young people, was looking for an adventure. Neil Capassa, a Canadian who was once a friar, was still in search of something, only God knows what, as he walked his fourth Camino (he was planning another for the following year). Kimberly from San Francisco had quit her career, traveled to Saint-Jean-Pied-de-Port, and started to walk. Wym, a 74-year-old Dutchman with visible signs of Parkinson's disease, had come to Saint-Jean-Pied-de-Port with his heavy-duty bike all the way from Maastricht in the Netherlands. Rene, also from Holland, had walked to the Pyrenees on foot from Rotterdam but had been ordered by a physician to rest for a full week due to severe tendonitis. Two women from Catania, Sicily, were convinced there has to be something better in life than getting up every morning and going to work. Christof read about the Camino de Santiago for the first time in the late 1992, when he came across Paolo Coelho's well-known book. Reading *The Pilgrimage* planted the seeds of desire to do this journey at some point in his life. Five years earlier he had carved himself a pilgrim's cane and placed it near the front door of his home in Berlin to remind him never ever to forget about his wish. Christof's desire to walk "The Way" remained for years. He longed to leave the daily battles of modern life behind for a period of time and live a more simple life that involved only sufficient food and water during the day and a shelter for the night. The *peregrinas* and I met Christof at Orisson Refuge in the Pyrenees. We became close friends during our journey through Spain and our quest to reach Santiago. Brigitte, from Koblenz, Germany, was a walking addict, to put it mildly. She could walk 30 miles a day with ease. She had competed in the 2003 Trans Europe Footrace from Lisbon to Moscow, 5,100 kilometers! She had even been a favorite to win the race! She had climbed Mount Kilimanjaro in Africa and Aconcagua in the Andes and had participated in many other competitions such as the Swiss

Alpine Marathon in Davos. This was amazing to me; Brigitte was 60 years old. She talked as fast and as much as she walked. None of us could keep up with her. Connie and Marianne, or the Swiss Misses, as I nicknamed them, were "soft pilgrims"; they spent nights in private hotels and had their belongings shipped via courier service to their next destination. Miché, from Pretoria, South Africa, already walked some 450 miles from Vézeley, France, on the Via Lemovicensis, one of the 250 plus Caminos in Europe; all of them ending in Santiago. Pascale, a short French Canadian with a sparkling personality, had walked along the Via Podiensis, starting in Le Puy-en-Vélais in France.

Saint Jean Pied de Port – France

We began our pilgrimage on Friday, June 10th, the day the three of us had arrived at Saint-Jean-Pied-de-Port from San Antonio. We had missed our last connecting outbound train in Bayonne; all the trains were late that day in France for some reason. The taxi we hired wasn't exactly cheap, but we wanted to get to our destination after a very long day of travel from Texas. The next morning, refreshed and rested, we had enough time to see and explore the small city, get our credentials at the pilgrims' office, and do some last-minute shopping for items we might need on the trail. Early Sunday morning, on June 12th, awakened by sounds of beautiful Gregorian chant at the Auberge L'ésprit du Chemin, Francesca, Valerie, and I took the first step on the Camino. We left the *auberge* and started our way up the Pyrenees to the Orisson Refuge with dozens of other pilgrims.

Refuge Orrison

None of us felt great that morning; the incline was steep. In addition, I was suffering from a self-inflicted upset stomach caused by the breaded fried pig feet and *piperade* (pepper sauce) I had eaten the night before to feed my obsession with trying the local Basque cuisine. This first stage made us wonder if we would be able to complete 500 miles. We met Christof and Neil for the first time as we reached Orisson. After a cold beverage on the *auberge*'s sun porch, we began the nightly routine we followed for the rest of the journey. It began with getting a fresh set of clothes ready, taking a shower, washing our sweaty clothes, and hanging them up, hoping they would dry in time. Valerie and Francesca, whom I had nicknamed my *peregrinas*, started a journal of their thoughts and experiences on the Camino. A lovely dinner, although it was pork again, topped off the evening at the refuge. On our second day we continued up the Pyrenees, using the route Napoleon had traveled, one with rugged trails and two passes, and then walked along the border between France and Spain. This was one of the most picturesque and rewarding stages of the entire journey.

Crossing the Pyrenees

The Col de Lepoeder with its view down to the monastery in Roncesvalles, Spain, filled us with great satisfaction. We felt very proud to have crossed the Pyrenees, a big first step indeed. We spent our first night in Spain in a monastery. The next two days were hot and clear as we walked 43 kilometers to the first major city, with one night's rest in the small village of Zubiri. Our group of friends broke the *peregrino* menu routine with delicious *tapas* and cold beer in the old part of the city of Pamplona. Some of our friends reminded me of my fast pace. "Why was I walking so fast?" I asked myself. Was I anxious about not reaching Santiago in time or was I still in the mode of my high-stress professional life? In my profession, everything has to be timely and perfect! My persistence sometimes created tensions with my two *peregrina* companions, and the warnings of fellow pilgrims were justified.

Much cooler temperatures prevailed as we climbed up the long and at times strenuous trail to the Alto de Perdón, or Height of Forgiveness, with its many noisy giant windmills and iron statues representing pilgrims. From the Alto, a gentle descent to Puente la Reina led us through lush fields of asparagus and artichoke and along a winding trail edged with aromatic wild fennel. The Hotel Jakue in the small city of Puente la Reina offered us a much-needed change from the bunk beds of the *albergue*s. I had reserved private rooms for the three of us. The *peregrinas* were able to shower as long they wanted and had enough time to tend to their sore feet and developing blisters. The hotel's dinner buffet for pilgrims was excellent. I paid particular attention to the carve-your-own *jamón ibérico* (Iberian ham) and quickly violated my decision to stop eating pork for a while.

The next day we reached the small village of Lorca after only 13 short kilometers in perfect weather conditions—clear blue skies and just-right temperatures. As we entered Lorca, we caught up with Christof and met Marianne and Connie, both of whom were rehydrating inside a small bodega. Neil and I ended that evening with a few too many glasses of Rioja. The next morning, we said goodbye to our gracious host Jose Ramon, sipped on a *cortado* (espresso with warm milk), and enjoyed freshly baked croissants that had just been delivered by the village baker. Our journey that day was one of the longer stages on the Camino, and we arrived in the late afternoon at Los Arcos. We felt good and tired, proud of our physical strength. The arduous 31-kilometer hike in 100-degree temperatures through many barley fields and elevations had given us a sobering taste of what was to come. The next day we traveled another hot and steamy 28 kilometers and reached that important 100-mile mark. That evening, we reached Logroño.

Francesca at the wine fountain at Bodega Irrache

We settled in and enjoyed a good night's sleep at the *albergue* Caminante in Belorado. Early morning, all of us, Neil, Francesca, Valerie and I, walked or limped to the bus station to travel to Burgos. When we arrived, we walked the short distance to the cathedral plaza. The Hotel Meson El Cid, located next to the massive and impressive Cathedral of Burgos, offered nice and quiet facilities. It all looked great, so we reserved rooms for three nights and looked forward to a long weekend that would allow our tired, injured, and stressed bodies to heal and recuperate. We rested, ate good meals, visited the cathedral, and took hundreds of pictures. Neil was nowhere to be found; we had lost the "Camino Ghost" again, as we called him. He must have checked into an *albergue* somewhere. Where were all the others, our Camino partners? It seemed like we had lost them all in that large city. As we sat at one of the many outdoor cafés at the cathedral plaza on our last evening in Burgos, the Swiss Misses showed up. Connie and Marianne finished their Camino in Burgos and we all celebrated their last evening with a dinner.

Early Monday morning, June 27, we resumed walking from Burgos, rested and refreshed. My vertigo was completely gone and the *peregrinas* were all bandaged up but very determined to take on the hot and endless Spanish highland, "the Meseta." We spent the next night in a bedbug-infested *albergue* in Hornillos del Camino. We left that place (with a few bites) before sunrise and walked the long 20 kilometers to Castrojeriz. The sun was merciless, and there were no trees, no shade. As we entered Castrojeriz, with its ruins of an old castle on top of a high hill, we agreed that private rooms were a must after our experience of the night before. We spent the night at the private Hostal El Manzano. Our dinner that evening at the only hotel in Castrojeriz was as good as most of evening meals we had on our sojourn. Everyone was happy to eat what was served. A heavy and very refreshing thundershower lowered temperatures for the night.

A room with a view in Castrojeriz

We caught up with Christof again 330 kilometers into the Camino and still inside the high plains, near Boadilla del Camino. He was looking for some fresh cold water at the same *fuente* (spring) as we were. We sat down for some refreshments inside the lovely courtyard at the En el Camino Albergue. Christof must have walked only a short way in front of us ever since we had left Burgos. He was a great source of knowledge of the Camino, in true Teutonic fashion. He was always fluent with details, from where you might get a free glass of wine to the condition of the terrain ahead of us and the many alternate routes to choose from. We stayed together for the remaining six kilometers to Fromísta, our destination for the night.

Much cooler weather moved in the following day on the seemingly endless and straight trail next to the highway as we walked to Carrión de los Condes. A large street sign on the main road reminded us of the 463 kilometers to Santiago. The push to Léon was on. Our next stop in a brand-new *albergue* in Terradillos de los Templarios marked the halfway point of the Camino. On Sunday, July 3rd, my birthday, I walked by myself into the city of Léon. Both of the *peregrinas* had too many foot ailments to walk and traveled the short stretch from Mansilla de las Mulas to Léon by bus and checked into a hotel there. Christof arrived a few hours later. We relaxed at one of the many outdoor cafés of this attractive city and then celebrated the night with some champagne and a nice seafood dinner in one of Léon's restaurants. Afterward, Christof and I consumed two or three glasses of Martini & Rossi wine before switching to gin and tonics at the Hotel Paris bar, the downtown hotel, where we all spent the night.

An alternate route brought us to our next stop, the small village of Villar de Mazarife. Reinhardt, an Austrian freelance journalist whom we had met briefly at Carrión de los Condes, was relaxing already in a comfortable lounge chair at the Albergue San Antonio de Padua. How could he be here already, I wondered, with his heavy limp? He had reached Mazarife by bus. We broke out in laughter when he told us of the 25 kilometers he had walked in the wrong direction a few days earlier and the difficulties he had encountered in his efforts to find his way back to the Camino. It can get confusing if you do not pay attention to the yellow arrows and scallop shells along the trail, but 25 kilometers? His mind must have been somewhere else. Reinhardt had a great sense of humor, but he knew that Mazarife meant the end of his attempt to finish the Camino. He simply could not make it any further with his injured and heavily bandaged knees. On our early morning start to Hospital de Orbigo, we said good-bye to our Austrian friend; he was waiting for the bus that would take him back to Léon. His Camino had ended.

Catedral episcopal at Astorga

Astorga is an important intersection, where Via de la Plata, which starts in Sevilla, merges with the Camino Frances, a lively city that features the beautiful Palacio Episcopal, designed by the famous Spanish architect Antoni Gaudi. We spent the night at the Albergue San Javier and enjoyed a delicious *peregrino* dinner in the dining room of the historic Gaudi Hotel. Earlier that day, we had bought cell phones so we could communicate with each other. Christof and I separated from the *peregrinas* and considered increasing the number of kilometers we walked each day; not exactly what the doctor suggested to me in Grañon! Soon I received my second lesson in how the Camino manages you, not the other way around. A gentle rise in elevation brought us from Astorga to Rabanal, where we stopped for some coffee and empanadas. The fireplace was already lit at a pit stop on the trail, and we noticed the cooler temperatures as we began our ascent to Foncebadon. Christof began to tell me about the many stories of the wild dogs of Foncebadon, where free roaming dogs have supposedly attacked pilgrims in the past. I believed it when I walked into that strange and abandoned-looking village, where many of the old houses were missing their roofs. It reminded me of an abandoned mining town. Fog and chilly winds moved in as we reached the halfway point between Rabanal and Foncebadon. I was sweating as I hiked uphill, and I suddenly felt very chilled. The perspiration on my body was turning ice cold, and I realized that my windbreaker was proving useless because I had no warm sweater underneath. Shivering and craving a hot cup of something, I paid the eight Euros for the night at the *albergue*. Minutes later I stepped into a hot shower and prayed the water would not turn cold on me. I put on a fresh set of dry clothes, wrapped myself in three blankets, and went straight to bed. It felt marvelous as my body started to warm up; and this in the middle of summer in Spain!

Marathon Brigitte was at the *albergue* too and brought me a large cup of hot tea. That was very thoughtful of her. She insisted that I eat some dinner. I had a few bites of the nicely prepared paella that I had smelled the moment I entered the *albergue*, then went back up to my bunk bed for a good night's sleep. As Christof and I walked to Molinaseca the following day, we placed our stone of sorrow on the existing pile at the Cruz del Ferro. The Iron cross is a powerful landmark on the Camino de Santiago, where you lay down a piece of stone you brought with you from home. On that site, two or three kilometers uphill from Foncebadon, every pilgrim stops to leave his or her sorrow behind, by placing that stone by the cross. Christof then shared a sip of Mirabelle schnapps he was carrying with him. It felt good and gave us the warmth we needed on that chilly morning. I was thinking of the *peregrinas*, who had spent the night in Rabanal. We figured they might be starting the ascent to Foncebadon by now. On the downhill trail, we met Miché again, the young lady from Pretoria, South Africa, who had started her journey at Vézeley, France. She had some 1,200 kilometers of trail behind her. The skies were covered with clouds that threatened rain, but we were able to see the city of Ponferrada in the far distance. The trail, which was full of sharp-edged rocks, was on a steep downhill slope. Christof tried to take a picture of me as I negotiated the steep, rocky trail. He focused his lens, but when he tried to click, I wasn't there anymore. "You just vanished," he told me later. I had slipped and fallen forward, but luckily the weight of my backpack had yanked me sharply to the right, and that had saved me from suffering a head injury. As I tumbled downhill over some nasty sharp rocks, I felt a sharp pain in my right knee. Miché was very quick at the site and found my glasses a few feet downhill. Christof reached for his first aid kit, ready to patch up my bleeding kneecap and elbow. I was lying with my head pointing downhill in a rather awkward position. Both of my companions feared I might have broken something. "You really must have a guardian angel. That was a nasty fall," Christof said as he administered first aid. I felt the sting on my knees as I slowly got up and wiped the dust off my clothes.

Cruz de ferro

Disregarding the pain, I walked for another 7 kilometers to Ponferrada, with a stop at a pharmacy in Molinaseca to clean my wounds again. Both my knees were hurting as we got closer to our destination. I knew I had been lucky and that it must have been fatigue that had caused the fall. Why hadn't I followed the doctor's advice? When would I learn that the Camino is not a foot race? Right then, I decided to take another day off before climbing O Cebreiro into Galicia. "It's time to pause," I thought. I had been on the journey for twenty-five days and had taken only two days rest.

As we walked along the paved street into Ponferrada, Christof talked about guardian angels and mentioned that if you visited a church, you might get some kind of answer about who your guardian angel might be. He was serious. I did go into the church in Ponferrada after we checked into a private hostel located next to a beautiful old Templar castle. I lit a candle and said a prayer. As I returned to our *albergue*, my cell phone lit up. It was my daughter Francesca. She and Valerie had made it to Molinaseca. "Dad, are you okay?" she asked. "I was thinking of you and worrying that something could happen to you on that steep trail down to Molinaseca!" How could she have had such an accurate perception of what had happened? She had no knowledge of my accident. Who had given her the message? Maybe it was a coincidence or perhaps it was the answer Christof had talked about.

We ordered pizza for dinner that night in one of the many restaurants along the main plaza, but we wished we hadn't. We were disappointed and knew that a simple *peregrino* menu would have been a much better choice in terms of both price and taste.

That's why we had an urge for a big, juicy steak as we arrived in Villafranca del Bierzo, the town I admired most along the Camino. After our usual chores, we walked to the Plaza Mayor and made ourselves comfortable at an outdoor restaurant, noticing the familiar smell of grilled meat. The owner started to brag about his incredible steaks, which had come from a 3,000-pound bull. "That's exactly what we are looking for," Christof said, and so did the three Frenchmen next to our table. Miché chose a seared tuna steak with baby eels. Those grilled sirloins were enormous, and so was the price. We also loved sipping the local wine made from Mencia grapes, which apparently only grow in the valley surrounding Villafranca del Bierzo.

Villafranca del Bierzo

Back at the Albergue de la Piedra, we treated ourselves to a foot massage. My wounds had started to heal well, although my oversized 28-ounce steak prevented me from having a good night's sleep. I purchased a nice warm sweater in Ponferrada, and we continued our way toward Galicia. We stopped at a small inn in Las Herrerias called El Capricho de Josana, the front door of which opens directly on the Camino. It was the perfect place for me to rest for a day and wait for the *peregrinas* to arrive. I called them to let them know where I was spending the night. Miché and Christof, slightly disappointed, went on to La Faba, some 3 kilometers uphill.

Knowing the girls had stayed overnight in Villafranca del Bierzo, I expected them to arrive at the inn in the early to midafternoon. As I sat on the stone wall along the Camino outside the entrance of the inn and waited for the ladies, enjoying the warm sun, the beautiful surroundings, and the magnificent view up to O Cebreiro, I heard a very familiar and distinct voice. For God's sake, it was Camino Ghost! Neil, carrying on with his usual and loud conversation about nothing, was walking toward me with some guys from Brazil. We gave each other a high five and talked for awhile. I had not seen Neil since Burgos. His knee seemed good again. They continued uphill to La Faba.

Valerie and Francesca soon arrived at the inn. After a fine dinner that night, a good rest, and a typical breakfast the next morning of fresh *pan tostada*, butter, and peach jelly, we were ready to climb the not-so-easy O Cebreiro and cross into Galicia.

El Capricho de Josana

We met Pascale early that morning coming out of a private hostel. She stayed with us all of the 30 kilometers to Triacastela. Heavy rain showers started as we entered La Faba. We hurried to cover our backpacks and rolled out the ponchos, then ordered a light snack at the café before resuming the uphill climb into Galicia. The rain kept pouring down on us. The trail turned muddy, the visibility was limited, and the winds were gusty. In La Laguna, everyone, bikers and hikers alike, piled into the only small café in the village to seek shelter. This must be Galicia, we concluded. It was the 12th of July and again logs of wood were burning in the restaurant's fireplace. We ordered tasty ham and eggs and watched the cold rain through the window as we warmed up by the cozy fire. We continued walking all the way to Triacastela as rain fell intermittently, reminding us constantly that we were in Galicia. In the midafternoon, we checked into the Albergue Complexo Xacobeo in Triacastela. The grilled lamb chops with ratatouille we had that night were delicious in the rustic and homey-looking restaurant next to our *albergue*. We rose early, and the three of us walked another 29 kilometers that took us through the city of Sarria, through lush green forests, and through landscape that resembled Ireland more than Galicia. We were happy with the occasional sunshine that broke through the clouds. By midafternoon we had reached our planned destination of Barbadelo and a modern, brand-new, lodge-style *albergue*, Casa Barbadelo.

After going through the physical phase at the start of our journey and the long mental stages as we walked the Meseta, we now experienced the spiritual phase of our pilgrimage. Santiago was so close! The days in the Pyrenees seemed so distant now. The next stage of our pilgrimage, which took us to a private hostel in the small farming village of Gonzar, brought us within 80 kilometers of Santiago. The place in Gonzar offered a nice courtyard and an equally nice bar, which I visited as soon as I arrived to quench my thirst. On our walk to Gonzar, we paused for a long lunch in Portomarín, where we ate a plate of Galicia's famous *pulpo*, then we climbed some more elevations. As we had so many times on the Camino, we could see our destination in the distance and thought we had made it, but we hadn't. We had to walk for another hour or more to finally reach the city of Palas de Rey. After a comfortable overnight stay at a city hotel in Palas de Rei, followed by a not-so-comfortable municipal *albergue* on our next stage in Ribadiso, we checked once more into a hotel in Rúa. I washed my clothes for the last time. The next day we would walk into the city of Santiago. It was the topic of our conversation during dinner that Sunday night in a neighborhood restaurant. One more day to go! The next 21 kilometers would be the last stage of our journey to Santiago de Compostela. That dinner marked our 35th walking day on the Camino.

The rain followed us during that last phase of our journey, as we passed Santiago's airport and climbed up to Monte del Gozo. From that vantage point, you should be able to see the towers of Santiago's cathedral, but drizzle and fog made it impossible that day. After Monte del Gozo, a monotonous walk in a steady drizzle ensued through Santiago's suburbs. We felt overwhelmed as we entered the Cathedral Plaza. The experience was very impressive and quiet emotional. The *peregrinas* had tears in their eyes. We watched the endless stream of pilgrims, bikers, and tourists reaching this final destination. Street musicians were on every corner. We had walked the entire Camino Francès. It was a moment we would never forget. We stood and looked around in silence. The three of us were standing next to the cathedral we had watched countless times on video clips before we began our journey. Christof and Miché had just left the cathedral; the daily Mass for pilgrims had just ended. Both of them found us quickly among the many arriving pilgrims. Pascale and even Marathon Brigitte showed up.

We checked into our hotel to freshen up and then visited Santiago's pilgrim office next door to have our credentials examined so we could receive our Compostela, the certificate that verified that we had completed our pilgrimage. At the dinner table that evening, we shared our stories and experiences from the past 36 days and toasted the successful end of the journey. Neil the Camino Ghost was missing again. "Who knows, the fool might be walking back to Saint-Jean-Pied-de-Port," someone jokingly remarked. We celebrated for two more days in Santiago, attended the Mass for pilgrims, and exchanged the *peregrino* menus and *bocadillos* (Spanish sandwiches) of the past weeks for Galicia's famous seafood and fine wine. Our friends Christof and Miché continued their journey all the way to Finisterre, the most western point of the Spanish peninsula, a spot that was believed to be the end of the world some 1,000 years ago.

Christof at Finisterre

Shopping was on our schedule the next morning. We ordered our usual *café cortado* at the bar in the hotel lobby and walked to the outdoor tables in front of the hotel. The Camino Ghost was sitting there, sipping a cup of coffee, waiting to say good-bye to us. On July 21st, we took a taxi from our hotel to the railroad station in Santiago for a trip to Madrid. We felt happy and sad as a huge curtain started to slowly close behind us. Part of our hearts will always remain on the other side of that curtain, on the Camino de Santiago.

Jubilant peregrinas at Santiago's Cathedral Plaza

2. My Culinary Education and Apprenticeship

Engelberg's Bellevue Hotel

My search for a culinary career began early, as did my passion for good food. It started at the age of 15, while I was working for an air conditioning firm, cleaning ventilation ducts in the kitchen of a well-known restaurant in my hometown of Lucerne. Observing chefs with tall hats as I stood on a ladder and cleaned the ducts fascinated me and marked the begin of my passion; to this day I still have it. It's got to be better than the work I was doing at the time, I argued to myself. However, it was not as easy as I imagined it would be. I was rejected at numerous places and I never heard back from others where I applied. Some of my job interviews did not go too well either. With my natural lack of patience, I started to feel frustration and anxiety. It was my father who finally found a suitable place for me at the popular mountain resort of Engelberg, some 35 kilometers south of my hometown. There is where my professional journey started, and I entered the workforce at the tender age of 16. I changed my temporary career of cleaning ducts to roasting ducks! As a spoiled kid from a sheltered home, I found myself surrounded with rambunctious cooks and *sous chefs* in some kind of hell's kitchen environment, with an executive chef who drank beer all day.

The Hotel Bellevue-Terminus, as its name indicates, is located across from the railroad terminal in Engelberg. It was an old and somewhat run-down structure that was owned by the Odermatt brothers, Adolf and Peter. My father drove me one afternoon in May 1959 from Lucerne to Engelberg and introduced me to the owners and the hotel's chef, an impressive middle-aged man named Hermann Cuonz who was from the city of Chur in southeastern Switzerland. For the first time in my life I was on my own.

I was shown to my room at the far end of the hotel, which was on the street level next to the laundry. The tiny room with iron bars outside the window reminded me of a jail cell. My orders were to be in the kitchen at 8 a.m. for breakfast, so I went to bed early, already worrying about being late. My first day on duty at the Hotel Bellevue was uneventful; I met all the cooks and *chefs de partie*, the *saucier*, the *entremetier*, the pastry chef, the *garde manager*, and the other apprentice, Guido, who already had one year of his education behind him. Guido made it clear to me from the get-go that he was the one in charge. I liked him, and we quickly became friends.

We all sat down for breakfast at the chef's table, which was very hierarchical. The chef was at the head; the *saucier*, who was the acting *sous chef*, sat to the chef's right; the pastry chef to the left; and all others further down the table. Guido and I were at the end, of course. Carla, a nice Italian lady from Naples who washed dishes, served a nice breakfast of freshly baked croissants, café au lait, butter, cheese, and marmalade. I noticed that the chef would not touch any breakfast, nor was he interested in the great-smelling coffee. Guido told me that the chef's calorie intake came in a different form, and soon I saw Carla serving him a big mug of beer. A cold brew at eight in the morning! Guido explained this was a daily ritual for our chef; he drank at least eight or nine mugs by 2 p.m., when lunch service ended.

Everyone worked a split shift, from 8 a.m. to 2 p.m. and from 5 p.m. to 9 p.m., six days a week, with Guido or I alternately on duty until 5 p.m. to serve the afternoon guests who came to our restaurant. By about 6:30 p.m., our workday was over.

Everyone returned for dinner service by 5 p.m. By that time, Chef Cuonz was usually wasted and was not functioning on all cylinders, and we would guess how many beers he had consumed during his afternoon break. Our *sous chef* then had to take command, working the counter to expedite all incoming orders. Poor Carla had to continuously provide beer for our chef. Over the following days and weeks, I noticed a lot of this going on, but no one really cared, nor was anything said or done about it. However, the chef's drinking affected my training. No one really talked to me or gave me any helpful directions. To whom could I turn besides Guido for guidance or questions? I found out quickly that it would not be the chef. Most of the other guys were bullies and seemed to get away with everything. I really wanted to be part of the work and show everyone that I had a keen desire to progress in this environment.

Discipline was nonexistent in that kitchen. Guido had much thicker skin than I did. He was able to stand up to the bullies quiet well. He was tall and strong and had a deep voice that worked to his advantage, but the close-knit clique that surrounded the chef found an easy target in me. I was a total greenhorn, and they had plenty of opportunities to tease me. Some days the boys would put me at the potato-peeling station, where over 100 pounds of unpeeled potatoes were stored in burlap sacks. My job was to peel them and put them in very large metal bowls filled with cold water. The culprits seemed to enjoy sneaking up behind me and throwing heavy objects like iron skillets into the water, each time getting me soaking wet. Other days they would make me count large containers of peeled onions over and over again, or I was given sacks of carrots to peel for the rest of the day. I really would have been quite all right with these tasks if they just would have left me alone. But I was labeled an idiot, a stupid "Stift" (a nickname for an apprentice). Or they would tell me things like "You'll never make it in this business because you're not bright enough and don't have the talent."

I guess the chef took pleasure in this, too. He must have noticed what was going on but never interfered; instead, he would devote himself to a fresh cold beer. Each night when I went to bed, I wept into my pillow, feeling very isolated and lonely. I was still a kid, and I had never been exposed to such an environment. Guido and our pastry chef, Reto, were the only fellows I was able to talk to. The teasing and abuse stopped one morning when Frau Hess, the coffee chef, came down to the kitchen. Frau Hess's title was *gouvernante*. She started her workday at four every morning, brewing fresh coffee, steaming milk, and preparing all the breakfasts. At lunchtime she operated the food elevator, unloading the meals sent up from the kitchen. She mastered a heavy workload every day but always offered a big smile and a kind word.

Once or twice a day, she would pass by our area from her upstairs service pantry to visit the storeroom to get silverware or other utensils and the provisions she needed for her job that day. One day she saw the chefs throwing big potatoes from their work station into water so it would splash onto me; they had found a new way to get me wet without sneaking up behind me. When Frau Hess saw what was going on, she stopped the nonsense and let the troublemakers have it. It was very gratifying to have someone looking out for me. But then I started to worry that the instigators will get mad at me and retaliate. The potato throwing stopped, but the verbal abuse continued.

Early in July, the chef's wife, a lovely lady, came for a visit. Our guess was that she was concerned about her husband's drinking. Guido told me a secret about the chef: his entire salary went directly to his wife, and he was left with only pocket change each month. When he was broke again, he would start to borrow money from us! Guido's salary was 20 Swiss francs per month; mine was only 10 francs. By the end of June, the chef had started to hit me up for my meager 10 francs. I was happy to give what I had left, hoping things would get better. How naïve I was! When the next payday came, he did not pay me back as he had promised, and of course I was afraid to ask him. The same thing happened with Guido. I actually began to believe this was normal, that this must be a regular practice at our hotel. I started to feel a strong resentment toward the chef and some of the lead chefs.

Peter Odermatt, the general manager, entertained his favorite guests most nights, and his brother, Dr. Adolf Odermatt, who had a PhD in economics, was mostly busy restraining his wife Ruth, a former model who frequently acted out after having a few too many drinks at the hotel bar. One early weekend morning, a loud commotion outside my iron-gated window woke me up. The good doctor was dragging his half-clothed wife Ruth toward their villa, which was behind the tennis courts. She kept swinging her purse at him while shouting obscenities. They had come from a nearby chalet that was the residence of her ex-husband. I could not fall asleep again after that incident. The dreadful thought of walking down the long hallway to the kitchen in a few hours kept me awake. The pastry chef tried on many occasions to encourage me to pull through and disregard the bullies. He meant well, but he could not do much about the situation because our German *sous-chef* quickly retaliated if someone told him something he did not like. I noticed that even the chef was afraid of him.

By the end of July, I couldn't take it anymore. The comfortable shelter I had enjoyed at home was no more. Even though my parents somehow kept a close eye on me, I felt frightened, hopeless, and alone at the hotel. Was there a way out? This question had been going through my mind for some time now.

One evening I told Guido and Reto that I was planning to quit. "What are you going to do?" they asked me. "You're on a contract for five entire seasons. Talk to your parents about it first." I knew that I couldn't do that. I tried to explain to my friends that I wouldn't have the courage to disappoint my parents after they had finally found a place for me. "Eddie, you are crazy; if you walk out, you have to go home anyhow and face your parents, so why not tell them now?" I knew they were right, but there was no way I could go home and see my Mom cry. "How about your brother, your sister?" my friends asked. My sister Vreni was studying in Paris at the time, and I didn't really know my 22-year-old brother. We hadn't grown up together, and he probably would think that I'd lost all my marbles if I told him of my plans.

Perhaps my godfather in Erstfeld would understand my dilemma. I remembered him as a very gentle and easygoing man. He would understand my problem. But how would I get there? By train? By bus? Hitchhiking? I told Reto that I was broke, that chef had asked me to advance him my money and had not paid me back and that I didn't think he ever would. "There's a shorter way to get there," I said. Both my friends looked at me askance. "How?" "Surenen Pass," I said. Guido and Reto were alarmed at this suggestion and were convinced that I had totally lost it. "That's at least a 30 kilometer hike over the mountains! This could be dangerous!" Reto shouted. "I am leaving early tomorrow morning," I insisted, "and please don't tell anybody, except Frau Hess later in the day. She needs to know."

On Monday, July 27, 1959, a gorgeous warm summer day, I was on my way to nowhere, depressed and confused. At 5 a.m., I left my room, dressed in shorts, a light shirt, and inappropriate shoes. I had no money in my pocket. All I had was a knapsack, two sandwiches, some fruit, and a one-and-a-half-liter bottle of water. Reto had smuggled all of it to my room at four in the morning. "Hurry, Eddie, before somebody sees you," Reto whispered. "The sun is rising soon; get out of here in the cover of darkness." I left by the north end of the hotel, which put me on a trail that passed by a nearby monastery. As I walked by, I saw some monks watering the beautiful flower garden on the premises.

I began to realize how difficult the hike over the mountain pass would be. The trail was a section of the Via Alpina that crossed over Switzerland from Vaduz, Liechtenstein, and then on to Montreux. My destination was Erstfeld, Canton Uri, in the Reuss Valley. The ascent began and the majestic Spannort Mountains seemed to come closer and closer. I stopped at Alpenroesli, the last small restaurant on the trail. The place wasn't open yet, and the sun was still hidden behind mountains, but I filled my bottle with fresh cold water and ate both sandwiches; with no breakfast I was very hungry after hiking for ninety minutes. The harmonic sound of cowbells and rushing mountain stream from the Spannort glacier gave me a short moment of peace and the feeling of being free. It was such a gorgeous day.

Then I began to realize how unprepared I was for such a long mountain hike. But there was no turning back now. Very soon everyone at the hotel would be wondering where I was. If the weather turned, that could mean serious trouble because I had no shelter and no hiking gear. I kept on going, though; returning to Engelberg would be awful. I imagined the panic my mother would feel, when I realized that someone would have to notify her that I was missing from work. Angst and uncertainty began to preoccupy my mind as I continued my way up the rocky and winding trail. I had had very little sleep the night before, and I felt tired. The shoes I was wearing didn't help either. The trail became narrower and steeper. I stopped and leaned on a large rock and ate some of the fruit and drank the remaining water. There was no one else on the trail. All I could hear was the sound of cowbells. I continued ascending and reached the timberline, and finally I reached the summit, at 7,600 feet above sea level. I didn't have a watch, but I knew I had been hiking for at least several hours.

Reaching the top of the mountain was a big relief and I remained hopeful that I could make it to Erstfeld before nightfall. I searched for the trailhead leading to Erstfeld and discovered it about two kilometers past the summit. I began a very steep descent, from 7,600 feet to 500 feet, and soon I had blisters on the bottoms of my feet. The trail was not well marked and patches of snow confused my sense of direction. Suddenly I was standing on a spot where I could not go in any direction: a cliff was in front of me and a steep ravine was to my right. I was still above the timberline. I was hungry and thirsty, I had no water or food left, and I was afraid that I would get lost. I backtracked about 150 meters, trying to locate the trail again. Suddenly I saw another hiker, the first human being I had seen since I left Engelberg. The young lady hiker was dressed in full hiking gear, traveling up the mountain. Relieved that I had finally made an encounter, I walked toward her. Surely she must have noticed how poorly outfitted I was. We stopped and talked for a few minutes. I was trying to tell her why I was up there in the first place. I do not recall her name but I remember her telling me that she was from Fribourg, in western Switzerland. She shared part of her water with me and gave me a few cookies and a candy bar. She also gave me five francs and pointed me to the trail down to Erstfeld. She must have been an angel! I was so grateful and still think of her often.

    I limped into Erstfeld, exhausted after a rather steep descent through the forests. It must have been around 6 p.m. My feet were very sore. I was looking for my godfather, who lived somewhere in the village in a small house and worked as a conductor for the Swiss railroad. We saw each other at the same time as I dragged myself through the village. He was still in his railroad uniform, and he shouted "Thank god you're here!" He had been alerted that I was coming his way and had been walking through the village to look for me. We walked together to his house, where his wife administered first aid to my feet, then prepared some sandwiches and hot tea. My godfather quickly called the local Alpine rescue station to report that I had arrived and was safe.

    I learned later that Frau Hess was off that day and that Reto and Guido had broken their silence after lunch, when they learned that the hotel had informed my parents that I was missing. Dr.

Odermatt, who happened to be the head of the Alpine rescue squad in Engelberg, had been ordered to begin a search and rescue by 6 p.m. from the Engelberg side; a similar search would begin at 7 p.m. from Erstfeld. Good luck was on my side, and everything was called off in time. I am sure the chef at the hotel poured himself another cold mug of beer to celebrate.

My Dad arrived in Erstfeld that same day after nightfall. To my surprise he was calm, in fact even glad to see me. We talked for some time and he wanted to know exactly what had prompted me to do such a stupid thing. As a seasoned hiker and alpinist, he knew only too well that I could have become disoriented up there if the weather conditions had changed. This can happen very quickly in the mountains. I knew he wanted to teach me, as he had many times before, to have better respect for remote trails and be aware of their dangers. As a member of the Sierra Club and one of six survivors of a terrible avalanche tragedy in 1921 in which he had lost seven of his closest friends, he knew what he was talking about.

Dad suggested that I stay at my godfather's house for a few days to relax and think about my future. Soon after our talk, he left for Lucerne. I went to bed, trying to digest the conversation. The eleven-hour hike put me to sleep quickly. Late the next morning, a strong smell of roasted cabbage woke me up. A hot shower and a set of fresh clothes that my Dad had brought along the night before made me feel like a normal human being again, although my blistered feet needed some more attention. When Alois, my godfather, came home for his two-hour lunch break, all of us had a delicious lunch. His wife had prepared a fine local specialty: pork stew with cabbage. She served me a bottle of my favorite soft drink with the meal. My godfather arranged a one-way ticket for me and sent me off to Lucerne.

At home, Dad made it clear that he expected me to finish my apprenticeship and culinary school. My mother was crying, of course. I felt very guilty and the thought of facing the people at the hotel again made me feel uneasy and troubled. We returned to

Engelberg on Saturday, August 1st. My Dad's diplomatic skills returned me back to work and almost everyone at the hotel was glad to see me safe and back on duty again. Frau Hess was especially happy; I knew that she had been worried about me. Guido and Reto gave me a warm welcome. Dr Odermatt smiled at me when he saw me return with my Dad. He said, "You were lucky that you had good weather; it can be dangerous up there!" He tried to be nice about it.

My dangerous and ill-planned adventure did bring some positive changes. Mr. Cuonz was no longer served cold brew by Carla. I learned that after several seasons at the Bellevue Hotel, his contract would not be renewed. He had about five or six weeks left in his employment. The bullies in the kitchen were quiet and chose to ignore me for the rest of the season. None of them was rehired for the following season. Things definitely were looking up.

The following October, I began two intense months of culinary school in Walchwil on the shores of Lake Zug. My training took place in a nice small resort hotel with renowned restaurant and banquet facilities. These were much better times, and I started to enjoy my work as I continued to grow up. Our instructor was one of the well-known chefs at the time, Henry Jolidon, the executive chef at the Gstaad Palace, which is still one of the best-known hotels in the world.

The Palace in Gstaad

Jolidon was a very sociable individual and loved good food, good wine, and good cigars. On many chilly November evenings, we watched Henry light one of his fine cigars that he had previously soaked with an equally fine cognac and then slowly dried over the warm wood fire oven in the restaurant. He told us stories about his travels and his career at the Palace Hotel in Gstaad while savoring his cognac-infused Monte Cristo. He relentlessly pounded the idea that there is never a substitute for quality into our heads. It had an indoctrinating affect on all of us students. I still can hear him today. We learned much about wines too, since the owner of the resort was a truly great wine expert who was never hesitant to open some of his finest bottles, all covered with dust, from his cool wine cellar. The chef for the resort was a very creative young Swiss professional who encouraged us to be more introspective, something I desperately needed. Unfortunately, school ended abruptly sometime in late

November, a week earlier than scheduled. Most of the students, including me, suddenly became ill with fever and general weakness. Every day a few more of us experienced the same fate. The owners of the resort called in a local physician and the Health Department. Leptospirosis was the diagnosis. All of us were ordered to go home and seek a doctor's care. The school closed its doors. It took me weeks to recover.

In 2008 as I traveled to Gstaad to attend the wedding ceremony of my friends Tom Russell and Nadine von Däniken, I had hoped to maybe see and visit the old master, but I learned from the present executive chef at the Palace Peter Wyss, that Henry Jolidon had passed away.

I returned to Engelberg in January of 1960, healthy again and full of enthusiasm for my second season. There I met the new chef, Mr. Lorenz Rubis, a great educator. He also had a good handle on the new staff and quickly restored discipline in the kitchen, which was so urgently needed. I was assigned to *tournant* (relief) duties for the winter, which gave me the opportunity to work in all areas of the kitchen. My shattered confidence from my first season started to fade; there was no more weeping into the pillow, no more peeling potatoes and carrots for ten hours, no more counting onions. My new room assignment on the top floor of the hotel was a very welcome change from the jail cell. I had plenty of reasons to be happy about and thankful for the changes.

The summer season of 1960 started in May. That season, I grew professionally and developed better skills. My summer assignment landed me in the *garde manger*, where everything cold is prepared and processed. In a large operation, there might be a butcher or meat cutter on the payroll. Our hotel would not support such a position, and I was excited to have the opportunity to learn that part of our profession.

So, I began my third season with a massive increase from twenty to thirty Swiss francs per month. I began to like my duties as the meat cutter. I boned veal, beef, and pork and prepared all the cold dishes for the hotel. This gave me the opportunity to plan ahead and then try to manage the workload. This was an area in which I failed on numerous occasions. The planning always worked well, but when it came to the execution, I experienced acute "labor pains." Chef Rubis was often less than enthusiastic about my performance, but he was always there to coach me out of the mess.

One Saturday night that summer, Dr. Odermatt's wife Ruth was on one of her drinking sprees. I happened to be on guard duty for the restaurant. I noticed her entering the kitchen from the bar, then lost track of her, since I had a few orders to take care of. I figured that she was hungry after all the booze she had consumed. Between the *garde manger* and the pastry area, we cooled leftover food from the dinner service in bowls and hotel pans before we transferred it to the walk-in refrigerators. I went back there to look for her, but I was too late. She had a spoon in her hand and had obviously aimed for a bowl of leftover mashed potatoes but had lost her balance while bending over to see what was in the bowls. Her face was buried in mashed potatoes. She tried to stand up straight, and what a sight it was! I ran for a bunch of napkins and handed them to her. She left the premises through the back door and disappeared into the hallway without saying a word.

Guido finished his apprenticeship at the end of that summer. He graduated and went on to better things. Unfortunately, we never heard from each other again. My third season came to an end and I stayed at the hotel until the end of October to feed the staff members who were left and do odd jobs throughout the property.

I attended culinary school for eight weeks that fall, this time at a small hotel owned and operated by the Siegrist family, the Seehotel Kastanienbaum. The hotel was a popular location for seminars and spas and was always a premiere destination for weddings. Its facilities were very nice. The hotel is located directly on Lake Lucerne and has a magnificent view of the Swiss Alps. It was an ideal site for our school and I was very close to home.

Special hygienic procedures were implemented that year to prevent another outbreak of infectious disease.

See Hotel Kastanienbaum

During eight-week term, I met my new chef instructor, Paul Rüegsegger, the executive chef of the Bürgenstock Hotels, three five-star luxury hotels that we could see across the lake from our windows. Rüegsegger became my mentor. Throughout my career as a chef I adapted some of his management style in the kitchens I worked in. He was a master of his métier and an outstanding administrator. Chef Rüegsegger was in charge of all three luxury hotels, the Grand Hotel, the Park Hotel and the Palace Hotel, and his culinary knowledge and style were exceptional. There was no doubt in my mind that one day I would work and learn in one of his kitchens.

Kastanienbaum was a good experience for me and also signaled the end of my formal schooling, although each of us still had to complete one more year of internship in our assigned hotel. My fourth season started in December of 1960, where I had to learn new skills at the stove, which meant learning everything about sauces, sautéing, roasting, grilling, and soups. I had to stay at the property over the three-week closure in the spring, doing add jobs like cleaning windows with Frau Hess. In June, my last and fifth season as an apprentice, I suddenly moved from an insecure kid who had run away over the mountains to the prestigious position of saucier. That must have been a good deal for the owners. 50 Swiss Francs per month, definitely inexpensive labor! At the end of the summer season in 1961, I had to prepare a three-course meal for eight to ten people as the capstone event of my formal education. I was very anxious about this because I wouldn't know what the menu might be until my instructors, an experienced chef from a reputable restaurant in Lucerne, and a hotel owner, also from Lucerne, arrived in Engelberg that morning. I prepared the *mise en place* the night before to ensure that all of the basics needed to prepare a menu would be ready. That saved my day. At eight in the morning, both instructors asked me to give them a tour of our facilities to determine my graduation menu. They were taking notes as we moved along. It made me nervous. We went to the restaurant and had some coffee while the instructors began to compose and finalize my menu. The hotel secretary rushed to her office and typed the menu on nice cards. The instructors gave me one of the cards. "Here it is; you have plenty of time. We would like to eat at 1 p.m.," the instructors said. Potage Pierre le Grand (cream of celery soup), Jarret de veau bourgeoise (braised whole veal shank with vegetables), and Crepes Normande (French apple crepes). Sounds easy to me today, but it wasn't then!

To my advantage, I was well prepared with almost everything I needed. One of the instructors was always watching over me; I was never alone. After the lunch was served, I found out that my ordeal wasn't over yet! The chef instructors explained to me that they usually get hungry again around 5 p.m. Both of them wanted something else to eat by early evening. That was a surprise! The dinner entrée the chefs assigned was filet of Dover sole in white wine sauce with fresh mushrooms, and garnished with fleurons. I had made this dish several times before and had no problems preparing it, although I was still nervous. They also wanted to test my skill in filleting a whole piece of fish. I managed to get by, but I am still not very good at this job. It was a long day, but everything I prepared turned out well and satisfied the stomachs of my instructors. I received high marks. This was the end of my chef schooling, two-and-a-half years after I had run over the mountains.

My season continued for three more weeks. The hotel closed and I was once more stuck with cooking the meals for the owners and few remaining personnel. Some of them had special dishes they craved. As the weather turned chillier, Dr. Odermatt liked Alpen Magronen—his version, of course. And then there was Kaiserschmarrn. Boy, did I hate that dish! The mother of the

Odermatt brothers, who was 80 some years old, was a feisty Austrian lady named Susie, a true and sometimes charming Viennese. Like her sons, she had one particular favorite. Whenever she called with an urge for that specialty dessert, I knew I was in for a culinary lecture. Kaiserschmarrn is a traditional Viennese dessert like a caramelized pancake made with soaked raisins, flour, sugar, butter, and vanilla flavoring. The pancake is cut into pieces it is while frying in the pan, sprinkled generously with confectioner's sugar, and presented with a warm plum sauce. I do admit, it's very tasty, but I disliked it because Granny Odermatt always stood beside me and corrected me during each step. Her strong, harsh-sounding Viennese accent did not help. Sometimes I had to repeat the process two times until Frau Susie was satisfied with the outcome. As time went on, my Schmarrn improved, and that made Frau Susie very happy. I never really had a recipe; she always coached me through the process.

Despite the enormous difficulties I had experienced as I began my culinary career at this hotel, I decided to return for another season. I liked the way the chef, Mr. Rubis, was teaching and the discipline he maintained in his kitchen. Nothing else had changed when I returned for my sixth consecutive season, though. The Odermatt brothers and Ruth were still there, of course, and they continued to be the best customers of the establishment.

By that time, I actually liked working at the Bellevue Hotel. During the years I was there, I made a number of friends in the local community. One of them was Teddy Amstutz, whose mother directed the housekeeping department at the hotel. Teddy was an incredible skier; for a short time, he was a member of the Swiss Alpine Team. He was very popular with the ladies as well. His girlfriend, a very pretty blonde, managed the old Titlis Hotel. One year lucky Teddy got a brand-new Volvo from her as a Christmas present. Teddy showed off his new toy to me and his mother on New Year's Eve that year. It was a square, boxy-looking automobile. Since his girlfriend worked all night and could not celebrate the New Year with him, Teddy asked me to join him for a couple of drinks after I got off work. I agreed to meet him around 1 a.m. at a popular drinking establishment, the Bierlialp. The owner of this popular watering hole, Freddie Rilliet, carried at least 180 pounds of excess weight. He was a great entertainer and a very pleasant fellow to hang out with. We stayed until about 4 a.m. I had to get some sleep, since my workday started at 8 a.m. Teddy insisted on driving me to the hotel, which was not a very bright idea, since he had been drinking all night. Besides, it was only a five minute walk to the hotel. When we got to the parking area, a light snow was falling. I noticed Freddie locking the back door of the bar and realized that we were the last to leave the establishment. There was nobody in the streets, and the weather was icy, windy, and cold. It took Teddy only one minute on the icy surface to lose control of his brand-new toy, and we ended up at the entrance of a nice sporting goods store. The owner was no other than Teddy's uncle. The front door of the store was a bit damaged, and Teddy's new Volvo was missing a headlight. Teddy's uncle lived above the store and was awakened by the crash. Before he made it down, I left; the hotel was right across from the scene of the accident. I never heard anything more about it, and I never asked Teddy how he explained the incident to his girlfriend.

That year, our local hotel and restaurant employees participated in a giant slalom race. It came about during a discussion at one of our local union meetings. In one of the local traditions, many winter resorts organized an annual chefs vs. waiters hockey game. The waiters wore tuxedos, and the chefs dressed in full uniforms and tall chef hats. The local union boys wanted to do something different. At work that evening, I presented the idea of a slalom race to the only person who could make such an event possible, Dr. Odermatt, the director of the ski school in Engelberg. He had also been a member of Switzerland's Olympic ski team in 1948. He welcomed the idea with great enthusiasm. A date was set and I gathered possible participants from hotels and restaurants and begged our food purveyors to donate good, such as gift baskets. We recruited a couple of dozen participants for the event.

The race started on a weekday at noon, which was difficult because everyone was busy with their jobs, but most managers and owners were enthusiastic about the event and allowed their employees the time to participate. Dr. Odermatt and his ski instructors had staked out the giant slalom course. They had even set up Longines timing, which was very impressive. Light snow was falling that day. Teddy Amstutz was the first to run the giant slalom and was not timed. Everyone was excited to see him, since was a well known downhill racer at the time. I noticed that he was a much better skier than driver! Some pretty good competitors came down the hill. One of our very young dining room waiters was the winner; watching him master the giant slalom was very impressive. His timing was more than ten seconds faster than the runner-up! Hot chocolate and snacks were handed out at the finish line. We found out that our winner was not a novice ski racer; he had hopes of being selected for Austria's junior National Ski Team. We had a great celebration that night at a local hotel, where medals and other prizes were handed out. I can't say enough good things about Dr. Odermatt; he was a true community leader, always ready and glad to help. His expertise and resources made the race a fun event.

Of course the union boys took all the credit, and by the end of the season they had even accused me of stealing funds for the race and filed a complaint. Many local merchants donated chocolate, gift baskets and so forth, which we stored at the hotel with the permission of management. The boys accused me of keeping these donations for myself. A registered letter from the president of the union was delivered to me a couple of weeks after the race that referred to the accusations from the union members and asked me to pay money to reimburse the union for the "stolen goods." The only thing I could think to do was seek advice from Dr. Odermatt and Chef Rubis. Both of them were outraged by the union's tactics and advised me to call the president and ask him for an appointment so I could explain my side of the story and document the case. This I did, and I was able to meet with him the following week in Lucerne. The appointment took place in the early afternoon at the Hotel Montana in Lucerne, the headquarters of Union Helvetia. The president of Switzerland's Hotel and Restaurant Union, Dr. Portmann, welcomed me with great courtesy. I explained my side of the case and told him exactly what had taken place. He listened carefully, occasionally asking me a few questions. He got up from behind his desk and asked his secretary to bring us a beverage. From that moment on Dr. Portmann had nothing than praise for me; he said that he could not believe that they were trying to smear me with this accusation. Then he called Dr. Odermatt, saying "I want to tell him what a fine young lad you are, helping to organize such a nice event for employees." When Dr. Portmann got Dr. Odermatt on the line, I sensed that they knew each other. The call was courteous and short; Dr. Portmann assured my boss that he would have a serious conversation with the local boys in Engelberg and thanked him for his fine contribution to and involvement with the event. That was a very good day for me indeed. I was happy and relieved of all my worries, and I had not expected Dr. Portmann to be such a pleasant individual. He knew that I had an assignment in Locarno for the coming summer season, and he wanted my word that I would show up for the first local union meeting of the season there. "I'll be there too," he said with a smile. The apology from the union came quickly; Dr. Portmann ordered the president of our local to deliver it personally. The case was closed, but I never really understood what their motive was.

 Although I grew very comfortable in this community and felt like one of the locals, my three years in Engelberg had ended. I was aware of the many things I still had to learn and experience in my quest to become a chef.

3. A Young Chef in Switzerland

Rene, the *sous chef* in Engelberg, had convinced me to work a summer season with him in Locarno. The Esplanade Hotel is a converted sanatorium in the hills above Minusio, near Locarno in the Swiss canton of Ticino, the Italian-speaking part of Switzerland. When I arrived at the hotel in May of 1962, I met Rene, Chef Molinari, and the hotel's general manager. By late afternoon that day, I had settled in to my assigned room for the season, which I had to share with a co-worker. Rene asked me to join the culinary staff for dinner at 5 o'clock. The meal was excellent, and to my surprise bottles of homemade wine accompanied the food; it was a touch on the sour side but not bad at all. I was hungry and thirsty, so it didn't really matter. Homemade wine and large platters of delicious local cheese were daily features at the chef's table for the culinary crew throughout the season. The hotel employed numerous gardeners, who grew many vegetables and herbs, such as zucchini, tomatoes, carrots, sage, rosemary, oregano, and marjoram.

Starting a new job was never easy for me. Not knowing what to expect or if I would succeed always made me anxious. When I finally dozed off that first night at the Esplanade, I had nightmares of working in the kitchen and burning an oven full of meat and poultry and then being chased out of the kitchen by an angry chef. After I woke up, I thanked God that it was only a dream. Naturally, I had difficulties getting back to sleep and began to worry that I wouldn't wake up in time for my first day on the job.

Our guests at the hotel were mostly elderly folks who were hoping to find more sunshine in the south than north of the Alps.

We catered to tours, most of which arrived by bus from northern Europe, Germany, Denmark, Sweden, Finland, etc. One of my lasting memories at this place was of bus full of Finnish tourists, about forty of them, who stopped for lunch. Asparagus Milanaise with sliced prosciutto was one of their preselected courses. We served individual plates neatly arranged with four slices of prosciutto. Later, as I went to look for something in the dishwashing room, I noticed the plates coming back from our dining room to be washed. The only thing remaining on the plates were the tender asparagus tips! "Wow! Guess the Finns would rather stick with reindeer and lingonberries," I thought.

The owners of the hotel, which at the time was affiliated with the renowned Dolder Hotel in Zurich, sent one of their interns for a few weeks to gain some culinary experience. This fellow was a loudmouth and seemed to have an answer for everything. Chef Molinari put him on the *entremetier* station, where he prepared soups and vegetables, or everything that goes on a hot plate except the protein. My roommate was the one in charge of this area. As you looked through the kitchen's screened windows, you could see a tiny waterfall coming out of a rusty pipe in the steep hills behind the hotel. With serious faces we convinced the intern that our signature minestrone soup, which was on the menu that day, was to be made only with "natural" water from that source. It was a long tradition at the hotel, we explained to the novice. We handed him several empty buckets and watched him through the windows as he struggled up the hill and filled bucket after bucket with the unsafe water. It took him an hour to make it back to the kitchen with all the dirty water. To his unpleasant surprise, the minestrone was already simmering on the stove. Our intern was less talkative for the few weeks he had left in his learning assignment.

Pastry chef Gambrosio truly was a great talent, an easy going "Ticinese" who was tall and soft spoken. He was part of the team that had opened the Istanbul Hilton and had worked in several other five-star properties. During the off season, he taught at the renowned Richemont Bakery School in Lucerne. One afternoon, between shifts, Gambrosio invited me to his apartment, maybe a half a mile from the hotel, to meet his wife and baby son. One of the gardeners handed him a wooden crate of zucchini to take home. We both jumped on his Vespa, the wooden crate of veggies on his lap, and scooted down the hill toward the main street, which was always full of traffic in both directions. I don't know exactly how it happened, but the vegetable crate slipped from his lap and fell on his pedals. He lost all the zucchini and of course he lost control of his Vespa. We crossed the main street and went onto the sidewalk, bumping into a public telephone booth. To our amazement, we were unharmed. A guardian angel must have been with us, as there was plenty of traffic in both directions just before we crossed the busy street. Gambrosio and I made it to his apartment with a slightly damaged scooter and both of us visibly shaken up, and of course there was no zucchini on the dinner menu that evening.

Local purveyors and merchants came to visit Chef Molinari at least once a week to take orders and introduce new products. Aldo Zarro was one of them, the proprietor of a local specialty food store that featured fresh seafood and other delicatessen items. He was a short man in his early forties with very bushy eyebrows and an upbeat mood; he was always cheerful and smiling. He had the reputation of being a special friend to local chefs and cooks. He invited many of us to tour his business and then to visit his lovely home, where we were treated to some of his fine products and delicacies. He was a clever businessman; when Aldo showed up, everyone gathered around him with curiosity, and when Aldo spoke, everyone listened. What he said was always educational. For example, he taught us how to expertly fillet a whole fish.

I loved Locarno, the people I worked with, and the mild California-type climate. On some of my days off, I was able to hang out with my two cousins, Mario and Enrico, who lived just a short train ride away in Lugano. Ermelinda, a native of Milan who worked at the front desk of our hotel, was petite and very pretty. Her long black hair and brown eyes fascinated me. Maybe she noticed this, because she visited the kitchen more often than she should have. We had a strong attraction for each another. She loved risotto, and whenever we featured it on the menu, I made sure to bring her a taste of it at a location close to the employees' dining room. That didn't last long, because Chef Molinari caught me carrying a plate of risotto to our secret location. He must have been tipped off, and the encounter wasn't very pretty. As I turned the corner, expecting to see Ermelinda, I almost collided with our angry-looking chef who was standing there, asking me if that plate was meant for him. That was the end of courting my secret love with risotto. Ermelinda was sorry and afraid that I was in trouble. Molinari chewed me out, and the case was closed.

At about that time, I received mail from the Swiss Army that informed me that I had to have a physical and a medical examination. I arrived one early morning at the military compound in Losone, just outside of Ascona, the home of marine-like special army troops. After the day was over, I was assigned to do basic training with them, which meant I had to be in excellent physical condition when I returned to the area in February 1963.

The summer season ended at the Esplanade. My good friend Gambrosio had left early due to family problems. Shortly before I returned home to Lucerne, I was strolling along the Quai of Locarno and of course reminiscing about Ermelinda, who had left a few days earlier to go home to Italy. As I walked, I noticed Gambrosio sitting alone on a bench starring at the Lago Maggiore. He looked sad; he was not the same Gambrosio I knew. With a tearful voice he told me that his wife had left him for good. I sat with him on the bench, both of us remaining silent. A bad thing had happened to a very good man. We hugged each other and said good-bye. I never saw or heard from him again. There was one more thing for me to do. I wanted to say good-bye to our friend Aldo and thank him for the things we had learned from him that summer. I had promised him that I would see him before I left Locarno. He was not there, but his wife assured me that she would pass on the message. The following day, I left Locarno by rail to see my family in Lucerne, knowing I had to return soon to spend time in the army. As my train passed Erstfeld, I looked up to my left into the clouded mountains and had a vivid recollection of the twenty-mile hike I had made over Surenen Pass only three short years earlier.

My dream of two years earlier, while I was in culinary school at the Kastanienbaum resort, soon became a reality. In the spring of 1963, after I completed my seventeen weeks of basic training in the Swiss Army, I was hired as a *commis de cuisine* to Chef Rüegsegger's staff at the Grand Hotel in Bürgenstock. The view of Lake Lucerne and all the surrounding mountains makes this place absolutely magnificent. It was exciting to become a part of this world-renowned chain of hotels. Some historic facts about Bürgenstock: The Grand Hotel opened in 1873. In 1888, the year the original Park Hotel opened, the city's cable car system and waterworks were inaugurated. From 1900 to 1905, the famous Felsenweg was constructed. In 1904, the Hammetschwand elevator was inaugurated and the Palace Hotel opened. In 1925, Friederich Frey-Fürst purchased the Bürgenstock Hotels. In 1927, a golf course was constructed. In 1953, Fritz Frey assumed management of the Bürgenstock Hotels, creating a second generation of owners from the Frey family. In 1984, the Bürgenstock Club opened; it included a restaurant, a bar, a health center, and an indoor swimming pool. In 1985, third-generation owner Peter Frey assumed management of the Bürgenstock Hotels. In 1991, a newly renovated Park Hotel opened, offering all-year rather than seasonal service. When Friedrich Frey purchased the hotels in 1925, he wanted to prevent a foreign syndicate from building gambling casinos in Bürgenstock. Today, a corporation from Qatar owns the entire mountain and is implementing plans to restore it to its original greatness.

Bürgenstock Resort

It's hard to believe that it takes half a day to travel the sixteen or eighteen kilometers from Lucerne to the hotels. First, you travel by railway to Stansstad, then you continue by steamship to the ship docks at the foot of the mountain, and finally, you take the cable car in Bürgenstock to the hotels. The Grand Hotel and the Palace Hotel were the luxury flagships. They had irreplaceable art collections and room rates higher than the surrounding Swiss Alps.

Fresh out of military service, I arrived at this picturesque mountain resort full of expectation but also with a dose of respect; I realized that from now on I would be playing in a bigger league. When I arrived, I was assigned to a small room with two beds in housing above five or six guest garages. Bathrooms and showers were at the end of the hallway. Tony Peter, my roommate, arrived a day later. He was a tall, skinny fellow my age with a quiet nature and a steady grin on his face. We worked together for several seasons. Another new arrival was Michael Durrer from Basel, fresh out of culinary school. He was a bit overweight but was always jolly and very likeable. Freddie Riesen, from Bern, who always had an ingenious answer to everything, also joined us. We all became good buddies and working partners.

My first day began with meeting other team members. Jean Perrin, from Sion in the Canton Valais, was the acting *sous chef* and chef *saucier*. He was in charge of preparing all meat and seafood entrees and any hot first courses. It was not an easy task to execute Chef Rüegsegger's sophisticated menus. I was very pleased to become Jean's *commis*; I knew that I would learn and benefit from the experience. Sven Kundig, a Swiss, was *chef tournant* in charge of the swimming pool restaurant, which was an ideal spot for lunch when the weather permitted. Guests from all three hotels loved to eat at this luxurious open-air location with its famous underwater bar and its magnificent view of Lake Lucerne and the Swiss Alps. Alex, from Germany, was our *garde manger*. He had quite a workload. He was responsible for processing all meats and seafood, salads, cold sauces, terrines, and pates. And of course there were always many special demands from opinionated guests who felt they had expertise about food. He was the one in charge of putting together a cold buffet for our pool service each day. Alex had difficulties with Chef Rüegsegger for some reason. Five or six weeks into the season, Alex tore off his apron, called it a season, and walked away, a reminder of an old rule that the chef is always right in his kitchen.

Our pastry chef was also from Germany, and our *entremetier*, the vegetable and soup guy, was Swiss. Although he was a very nervous person, he was very efficient. Every night he prepared a fresh consommé, and each day for lunch service he prepared *rösti* potatoes made to order. He also was responsible for the bisques on our a la carte menu, each of which had to be prepared to order. Middle-aged Luigi from Milan was our personnel cook. He had a huge mustache and a heart of pure gold. He prepared some 100 meals every day for the employees, both lunch and dinner. Although the Grand Hotel had only 54 rooms, our employee count was around 100, including the management staff. One of Rüegsegger's top priorities was good-quality and plentiful food for all employees. He inspected all of it every single day. The antique coal stove in the old-fashioned kitchen at the Grand generated enormous heat, forcing us to change our uniforms twice a day. Just the task of shoveling coal to keep the stove hot was a strenuous exercise. Our chef reminded us constantly about this job, which we disliked very much.

Fritz Frey was the proprietor; we called him the king of the mountain. He once said in a newspaper interview that the art of managing great hotels is simply an extension of the task of running a private household efficiently. Mr. Frey was a tall, handsome man with gray hair. He was always on the move, mostly on his Vespa, going from one project to another. He was heavily involved in everyday operation of the hotel. In today's corporate world, there would be an army of managers doing the tasks this man did single-handedly. In a day's time, you could see him with the landscapers and gardeners, making sure that only genuine Alpine flora was used, or in the kitchen discussing new dishes with Chef Rüegsegger. In his office he himself drew up plans for future projects; he never had an architect on his payroll.

An incident I shall never forget happened one summer during an official state visit by Princess Margrethe of Denmark. Fritz Frey had offered his yacht to transport the royal luminaries, Swiss government officials, and invited guests to the cable car station leading up to the resort. The special guests were served aperitifs and small hors d'oeuvres during the short ride on the lake. The lunch menu was protocol and had been delivered to us from Bern. After dishing up the first course of poached Dover sole filets with prawns and a superb sauce, Tony and I had to carve the roasted strip sirloin for the entrée in the dining rooms at the Grand Hotel. As I was rushing to the hotel's front entrance, dressed in a fresh uniform with my carving knife wrapped in a towel, Fritz Frey stopped in front of me on his Vespa, wearing his usual attire of khaki pants and a shirt with its sleeves rolled up. I was somewhat surprised to see him, as I had assumed that he would be eating at the luncheon, since he had offered all of the facilities for the royal visit and owned the entire mountain. Somehow annoyed, he explained to me that "our lovely bureaucrats in Bern left me out from the invitation list. The press will hear about this tomorrow," he told me, half-frowning. "Well Eddie, I just work here," he said, and drove off. That was an embarrassing oversight and he was upset. I think he went down to the gardeners' headquarters to have lunch break with them.

Michael, Chef Rüegsegger, Tony and me
Plating the first course for the Danish Royalties

Many celebrities came every summer. Fresh mountain air, a magnificent view of the Swiss Alps and only the best in food, beverages, and service made Bürgenstock the place to meet, relax, and be seen. Among the regulars were Sophia Loren, Audrey Hepburn, Mel Ferrer, Sean Connery, and Shirley MacLaine. Famous mystery writer George Simenon came every summer, bringing a special vegetable oil that he passed on to us for preparing all of his special meals. Other celebrity guests included Rod Stewart, Otto Preminger, Helena Rubinstein, Prime Minister Karamanlis of Greece, Conrad Adenauer, and Prime Minister Ben Gurion of Israel.

Then we had our regulars, some of whom stayed half the season and some who stayed the entire summer, such as Mrs. Fromm, the widow of the producer of most German condoms. She was a very friendly elderly lady who carried her paralyzed dog every day on her afternoon walks. She had a weakness for roasted duck and ordered it once a week, always eating a whole bird for dinner. It always had to be carved tableside. Then we had the Ballys, founders and owners of a high-priced shoe factory in Switzerland. This old and crochety couple spent long periods with us every summer, mostly at the Grand Hotel. They requested that all their meals be prepared without salt, but when their specially prepared food was served, they always asked for salt shakers. Nobody liked them.

Every day, chef put one of us *commis* on dining room duty. A neatly arranged cold buffet with *charcuterie*, terrines, and pates; a set-up of smoked salmon and its condiments; an antipasti cart; and a large and heavy silver *voiture* with the hot entrée of the day were the daily features in addition to chef's menus, which were served from the kitchen. We had to wear a crisp and clean uniform and were directed by the maître d' to the table of any guest who requested the buffet.

One day our luncheon entrée was *bollito misto*, a northern Italian specialty made of boiled meats such as osso buco, veal tongue, and *zampone* (a stuffed pig foot) with poached beef marrow bones and condiments such as salsa verde, fruit *mostarda*, pickled cucumbers, and olive tapenade. Mr. Bally requested my presence and the entrée cart at his table, which I thought was unusual, since his salt-free meal had already been delivered earlier. But old Bally suddenly was very interested in the poached beef marrow bones. Unfortunately I had none left on the cart, but I assured him that I would immediately order some from the kitchen. Mr. Bally looked at me with his sour face and nodded. Knowing that I had to act quickly, before he became combative, I telephoned Chef Rüegsegger and told him of Bally's request and that I had no marrow bones left. The chef was very busy at his counter and yelled "I am out too!" and hung up. Returning to Mr. Bally's table, I cautiously and politely explained the situation and apologized for the inconvenience. He was visibly agitated.

Then, without my knowledge, Chef Rüegsegger quickly poached a half a dozen marrow bones without salt and had them rushed to Bally's table. As I was standing by the service area, waiting to be called to another table, old Bally got up from his seat, approached me with a red face, and called me a damn liar. He was so mad that he actually spit over the entrée cart parked beside me. It was a good thing the cover was down. He was loud too, prompting many guests to turn their heads to see the source of the commotion. My friend Werner Keusch, the chef de brigade, came to my rescue and explained to Mr. Bally what had happened. It was good that Keusch intervened, because I felt like punching the guy. When I told our chef of the incident, he said, "That's life at the Grand Hotel; better get used to it, Eddie." I promised myself never ever to buy a pair of Bally shoes as long as I lived.

Werner Keusch worked in the dining room. He was undeniably the hotel clown. Keusch, his last name, means "virgin" in English. He called me to a table with a party of four, all Catholic bishops who were visiting from the United States. They were intrigued with the aromatic smell and presentation of the *bollito misto*. As I pushed the cart to the clerics' table, Keusch said to me, "Watch this, Eddie!" He then launched into one of his favorite introductions: "Good afternoon, bishops; welcome to the Grand Hotel. My name is Keusch and I still am!"

In 1964, a brand-new kitchen was built during the winter months for the upcoming summer season. It was Chef Rüegsegger's new toy. It was equipped with all-electric features. The stove had a water bath in the middle and eight powerful flat electric plates on each side. In addition, there were brand-new stainless pots and pans with extra-heavy bottoms, custom made for electric stoves. The walls were covered with white tiles. We were especially excited about the custom-built charcoal grill. Of course all of us were very happy that we would never have to shovel coal again. The chef's office had a command panel on the wall that indicated which and how many electric plates were in use. He was able to turn off the switches remotely if he felt that something should not be in use. Talking about energy management! It was a wonderful change from the previous summer, when we had shoveled coal all day long, and most of all, it was so much cleaner. Chef Rüegsegger spent a lot more time in his office, playing with his new toy panel. Trust me; none of us had any objection to that.

That year, Sven did not return to the job he had held for several summers, and I got his job. Every morning at precisely 10:30, weather permitting, and of course exactly during our short lunch break, Arnold would show up with his little custom-built electric cart. This meant that our lunch break was over and we had to load all the foods for the daily luncheon onto the cart. Arnold (we called him Noldi) was a man of few words. You had to force a conversation with him, and then he said only what he had to. After we loaded the scrumptious salad bar and the cold buffets, the chefs in charge would jump on the cart for the short trip to the pool with Noldi at the wheel. He was always chewing on an old cigar. I always thought this could have been the reason he never talked much. In addition to the cold buffet, we featured hot entrées, *grillades*, specialty sausages, steaks, and burgers.

Our guests loved the setup. The norm for lunch was 100 to 130 covers. Sometimes we would have everything ready and then the unpredictable Alpine weather would change on us, which meant loading up the cart again and heading back to the hotel, where we would unload the cart and look for a way to salvage all the food. Our friend Noldi became an important partner in this catering service. His consistent punctuality reminded us of a Swiss clock.

It turned out to be a great summer with relatively nice weather conditions by Swiss standards. The pool service was hectic on warm sunny days. One of the special requests came from an elderly French lady, who asked for a complicated chilled eggplant dish. She kept on visiting the kitchen to teach all of us how to prepare this vegetarian dish. She wasn't particularly friendly and treated Chef Rüegsegger like a student. She seemed to know it all. She requested this eggplant dish maybe twice a week at the pool. I had to prepare the eggplant every day, because we never knew if the old crow would show up or not. I began to dislike this eggplant dish very much.

    Every day Bruna, our Italian kitchen helper, prepared our house specialty of fresh peach salad with raspberry coulis, a very refreshing cocktail that was very popular on warm sunny days. Audrey Hepburn and her husband Mel Ferrer dined at the pool frequently, as did Shirley MacLaine and Gianni Agnelli, the principal shareholder of Fiat. One hot and extremely busy summer day, our refrigeration unit went out. This was a potential disaster because of all the Luis Roederer Cristal and Beluga Caviar we had in storage. Who showed up and repaired it? Yes, no other than Fritz Frey. He was a skilled electrician and had that refrigeration up and running again in a very short time. He surely was a master of all trades.

    Mr. Frey had designed a swing door for the service area of the Grand Hotel to muffle the noise from that area. All the waiters hated it because they had to push it open with their feet. My friend Keusch, who should have known better, confronted Mr. Frey about the door. He asked who the designer was. "I really would like to meet that incompetent architect," Keusch said. "You are looking at him," Frey replied, visibly annoyed. Mister Big Mouth Keusch disappeared into the dining room rather quickly and was quiet for the rest of the night.

    At the end of the season, after the Grand Hotel was closed down, part of our crew, including me, were relocated to the Palace Hotel for the international Kraft Foods convention. The Palace was equipped with a multi-language system and had numerous interpreters on site. Some of the best banquet food I've ever seen was served during that convention. One dish in particular was Chef Rüegsegger's lobster soufflé, which was presented tableside by an army of waiters. For 140 people, that is not an easy task.

The soufflés were presented in large ramekins, two for each table of eight. Service had to be quick and precise before the soufflés shrank. That particular lunch service was one of the best examples of coordination between kitchen and service I've ever seen.

Tony of course found some time for mischief; he tried to tell our young apprentice to run over to the Park Hotel and borrow the soufflé pump. "My lobster soufflé does not seem to rise," he explained to the novice and told him to hurry before it was too late.

Kraft Foods brought some samples of new things for us to test and taste. One particular item still remains in my memory is a freeze-dried scampi, or baby lobster tail. It needed to be soaked in cold water for some time to reconstitute it. The taste of this product was incredibly delicious. I never heard or came across this product again.

There weren't many places to socialize at night after hours, and we were not motorized at the time and had few or no opportunities to get down the mountain to go to Lucerne or anywhere else. We felt isolated, and some of us had too much energy and needed some excitement. On several occasions, this led to mischief. Some very bright fellows emptied bottles of liquid soap into the fountain at the Plaza; you can imagine the foam the gardeners and cleanup crew had to deal with the following morning. Fritz Frey was furious about that incident and promised to fire the culprits immediately. In another incident, three of our waiters, all French men, were caught at the pool one night, preparing a late-night snack from the foods I kept in the refrigerator. Mr. Frey caught them in the act.

Another time Freddie and I and Tony, one of our waiters, closed the Taverne, a nearby restaurant and a favorite hangout for chefs and waiters after hours. When we decided not to observe its closing time at 12:30 a.m., we were promptly thrown out. Outside in the garden restaurant, I attempted to climb the façade of the building, knowing that all of the waitresses were housed above the restaurants. I had almost reached my goal when one of the windows suddenly opened and two of the waitresses began to spray me with high-pressure syphon bottles, especially my eyes and nose. Soaking wet, I let go, clinging to the gutter. As my buddies helped me down to the ground, the peripatetic Mr. Frey arrived on his scooter from nowhere, asking what was going on. I am almost sure that someone in the restaurant had contacted him, as the three of us had had the audacity to ignore closing hours. The waitresses, leaning out of the windows, were more than willing to tell Mr. Frey of my intentions. He looked at me with a smirk on his face and said, "You are an illogical fellow, Eddie. I could have given you the key to their rooms." And off he went. Realizing that he was also his own security chief of the mountain, I began walking back down the street to our sleeping quarters, wet and plenty embarrassed.

The nurse that summer was beautiful, although none of us knew her personally. She treated employees for minor accidents when the hotel physician was not there (he visited the resort three times a week). On the night of the employee gala at the end of the summer season, we gathered at a small hotel half a mile from our properties. Tony, Freddie, Harald (who was a newcomer from Germany that season), Michael (an apprentice), and I were at the bar, drinking beer and having a great time watching people. Freddie was crazy about the nurse and repeatedly asked her for a dance, which she politely declined each time. All of us watched Freddie with amusement, and I saw that devilish grin creep onto Toni's face. It looked to me as he was up to something. He was! After the event, we enjoyed another beer back at our sleeping quarters, where Freddie kept on talking about the nurse. He was in love. Tony implemented his evil plan by writing a letter to Freddie with the nurse's signature; since we did not know her first name, we invented one. From then on, she was "Silvia." The content of the letter to "Silvia" was something like this:

Dear Freddie,

My sincere apologies, Freddie, I regret very much declining your numerous invitations to dance. I declined only because I was with my girlfriend, who was visiting me from out of town. I felt bad when the night was over, and I decided to write to you. I feel strongly that both of us are attracted to each other. You are always on my mind. Please write me a note and just slip it halfway under my door. You know where I live, at the administrative building by the doctor's office. I am passionately awaiting your response.

Silvia

We addressed the letter to Freddie and mailed it to him. He received it the following day. He showed the letter to all of us wicked fellows, clearly in heaven, telling us, "That woman just loves me. She even knows my name!" He answered the letter and after dark slipped it under her door. Tony was worried that if Freddie pushed the letter all the way under her door, the fun would be over. We sent Martin, one of our apprentices, to retrieve it. He did, and we opened it. Freddie's response:

Liebe Silvia,

I cannot express to you how excited I am about your wonderful letter expressing your love for me. I fell in love the moment I saw you at the gala. Let's get together as soon as possible. This coming weekend, perhaps? I can't wait to see your gorgeous face.

Love Freddie

"Silvia's" reply to Freddie, written by Tony:

My wonderful Freddie,

A girlfriend of my from Basel is visiting on Saturday. We plan go to the Fuerigen Resort that Saturday night, and I really want to meet you there for sure. I am truly missing you and I want to dance the night away with you cheek to cheek and hold you in my arms. I will passionately wait for you.

Love Silvia

Again we postmarked the letter and mailed it. After Freddie received the letter, we could not talk to him anymore; he was floating in a different world. I began to feel sorry for him. This was malicious, and I was part of it. Had I suddenly become like the tormentors I had had to endure at the beginning of my apprenticeship? I was not cheerful about it anymore, and I asked myself how I would react if that happened to me. The Fuerigen Resort Hotel was approximately two and a half miles down the road from the Grand. Tony and Harald left early and went by motorcycle to the destination, waiting for Freddie to arrive. Freddie walked to the Fuerigen in the dark, all dressed up, smelling like a French prostitute. It took him over an hour to get there in the dark, but when he arrived, no "Silvia" was in sight! The boys should ended it right there, but they chose to continue the vicious game and told Freddie that "Silvia" had left a few minutes ago in a car with her girlfriend for the casino in Lucerne and wanted to make sure that Freddie knew that she wanted him to meet them there. Well, Freddie called for a taxi and off he went to Lucerne. We finally told him the following day; Tony must have run out of ideas. Freddie was heartbroken. It was days before he would speak to us again. I felt bad, but Tony had a grin on his face.

Another memorable incident from that summer happened in connection with the wedding festivities for the daughter of the Ringier family, the owners of Ringier AG, a large Swiss multinational media corporation that was founded in 1833. The wedding was a high-society event with some 300 invited guests, most of whom arrived the Thursday and Friday before the weekend celebration. The menu was very elaborate and typical of the sixties. It included Russian caviar, roasted saddle of veal Soubise, and of course a masterpiece of a wedding cake that our pastry chef Heinz had worked on painstakingly after hours for several weeks. The special foods had arrived early that week. On Thursday, we poached 150 lobsters, which had been shipped in from Helgoland, in a very aromatic court bouillon, for the classic first course of *"Hommard a la Parisienne"*. By Saturday noon, we had begun to assemble the first course in our *garde manger* while our *saucier* prepared a perfect saddle of veal with all its sauces and garnishes. Hired professionals, the maitre d', and the waiters had done a truly spectacular job of decorating the ballroom and lobby area with incredible floral centerpieces. The stage had been set up by the very popular Hazy Osterwald show band for entertainment.

As the dinner ceremony approached, tension grew among the kitchen and service staff. When Mr. Frey showed up in the kitchen, we all thought that he was merely making his usual rounds, but instead he delivered some disturbing news. The bride had fallen ill with a fever, and the physician on duty suspected appendicitis. I can still see the concerned face of our chef. Mr. Frey assured Chef Rüegsegger and the rest of us that the wedding would take place, so we continued working to meet our deadlines. A half an hour later, two uniformed police officers and Mr. Frey walked into our kitchen and went directly to the chef's office, closing the door behind them. We watched them through the glass windows and saw the chef's face change color. I said to Tony jokingly, "They are here to arrest you for all the bad sins you committed throughout the season." The meeting was short. The police officers and Mr. Frey left. Chef Rüegsegger opened his office door, stepped into the busy kitchen, and told everybody to stop and listen. Then he announced, "Gentlemen, the wedding is off!" We all looked at each other with disbelief. On his way to the resort, the groom, who was most likely late and in a hurry, had missed a curve in his high-powered sports car. He had lost control of his vehicle and collided with a tree. He was paralyzed from the neck down and the bride had appendicitis, and there was no event to celebrate! For some reason, this wedding was not meant to be. We ate very well at the chef's table for the next couple of days.

In 1966, my final season at the resort, it was pretty much repeat business. Georges Simenon was there with his family and his special vegetable oil, of course. The Ballys continued to order their salt-free meals, and Mrs. Fromm was there again to order roast duckling. She was still grieving the loss of her beloved dog, which had died during the winter. The dog must have been the only thing she had left in her life besides all the money. Prime Minister Karamanlis from Greece spent part of the summer again, but he ate in his suite. Our friend Keusch was the only waiter who ever served the prime minister.

The newcomers that year included a very friendly and polite middle-aged couple from Italy. They had many specialty food requests. He loved our food so much he overindulged himself the first week with his special menus. Then he spent a few days in bed eating bowls of oatmeal and sipping chamomile tea. Once he had recuperated, he would start his compulsive eating pattern again. Some of the special foods he always asked for were *zampone* with lentils and *fegattini in brodo*, a tasty chicken consommé with rice and chicken livers.

Shirley MacLaine returned for a few days' rest. She ordered wieners with potato salad the first night she was there. I liked her taste; that's exactly what I order on my visits to Switzerland. It is always one of my first meals! Emilio Colombo, who held a cabinet post in Italy's government and at the time was a rising star in Italian politics, came for two visits a week or two apart with a couple of other government officials and ordered grilled liver every single day. It had to be done with a special olive oil that was not very commonly used in Switzerland at the time.

Sophia Loren and Audrey Hepburn were the finest guests, always friendly to staff and never complicated in their culinary demands. 1966 was also the year of the long-anticipated FIFA World Cup in England. I owned a small black-and-white TV with antenna ears. All of us could not wait to see the opening game between Uruguay and England, so we hid the small TV behind some old produce boxes. We took this risk because Chef Rüegsegger had one of his rare evenings off. I didn't think he would have allowed us to follow the game, but he wasn't there, so what the hell! I thought. The game was played during the busy dinner hours and we watched it at the same time as we struggled with our incoming orders. When the general manager, Hans Gredig, made his rounds, he promptly spotted the TV. Too many of the guys were watching at one time, I guess. That did not go over well. After he found out it was my television set, he promised me that I would spend the rest of the season in the dish room if the TV was not removed in one minute, "and I mean one minute." That was the end of our sneaky attempt to watch the evening games of the World Cup. Mr. Gredig continued to visit the kitchen daily to make sure the TV was not there; he didn't trust me anymore. On top of that I received an additional ass-chewing from Chef Rüegsegger the following day.

That season, an event was scheduled at the cozy Golf Club House for Sophia Loren, when she came for a short break from a film shoot in Yugoslavia. I was assigned to manage the event, which made me nervous, even though I had done numerous parties at the golf club before. It supposed to be a very casual affair. Chef Rüegsegger went over the menu with me in detail. Our friend Noldi delivered some dried vines that Mr. Frey asked us to add to the grill to enhance the flavor of the beef, something the actress always wanted for any kind of grilled meat. Mr. Frey had arranged the dinner party in honor of the film diva, who was a close personal friend. Carlo Ponti, Sophia's husband, and astronaut John Glenn were also present that night.

The guests began to arrive. When the starlet arrived in her miniskirt with shiny hair reaching to her lower back, all of us stopped what we were doing. She looked absolutely sensational. I added some of the vines to the charcoal on the grill while the party enjoyed aperitifs and hors d'oeuvres. Chef Rüegsegger called to make sure I had everything I needed. The meal began with a typical variety of seasonal salads with vinaigrette dressing expertly prepared at tableside by Mario, our *chef de service*. I began grilling the three-inch-thick porterhouse steaks, which had been rubbed with coarse cracked peppercorn and fresh oregano. I added more of the vines to the fire, noticing the fine fragrance. But I had to pay close attention to the steaks, since the vines generated some flames. I couldn't afford to burn them now. The aromatic scent from the burning vines and the sizzling prime beef made all of us hungry. We promised ourselves that we would taste some of it later. The porterhouse steaks turned out flawless, just as Miss Loren had requested: crisp outside, rare and juicy inside. Mario served the freshly carved meat; two other waiters French-served creamed kernels of fresh corn, steamed asparagus, and roasted new potatoes with black truffles; and a delectable choron sauce was passed for the meat. A fine selection of Italian and Swiss cheeses and wedges of fresh pears, apricots, and peaches accompanied with thin slices of lightly toasted Italian bread followed the entrée. For dessert, Mario flamed a variety of seasonal berries, including local wild strawberries, while I scooped homemade vanilla ice cream. The pastry chef had baked a selection of delicious *mignardises* for the coffee service. After the dinner, Mario and I disappeared into the small service kitchen and dined on some tasty prime beef.

Sophia's Dinner gathering at the Golf Club

Our hotels began to close their doors late that summer. The season was winding down. The Taverne Restaurant remained open, and one of us had to help Chef Rüegsegger continue with the food service at the restaurant, as was usual at the end of every season. Although at this time of the season, there was little business during the week, there was always the potential for hectic and long weekends as tourists from everywhere visited the picturesque and popular mountain. None of us looked forward to being assigned to such duty. This season it was Tony's turn to relocate to the restaurant and stay for a few more weeks, but he had forgotten one important thing at the time; he was scheduled for three weeks of military service. He claimed to have forgotten about it and had to rush home to get his uniform, gun, and ammunition and report for duty. How convenient! I had been looking forward to a break and a few days off from a strenuous season. Suddenly it was my turn to replace Tony and join the chef.

I honestly did not remember this story, but Tony, with the usual grin all over his face, reminded me of it over dinner at an eatery on the San Antonio Riverwalk some 43 years later!

During the off season, we searched for suitable jobs in the cities, mostly during October and November. After I finished my first season at the Bürgenstock Hotels in 1963, a few restaurant owners visited the resort to recruit some of us who were looking for such jobs. I agreed to go to work in Zurich. There are numerous guilds in Switzerland's largest city that date back to the fourteenth century. These guilds still exist today and have genuinely fine restaurants in this city. The Zunfthaus zur Schmieden was located right at the edge of Zurich's Niederdorf at the Marktgasse, the old town with its numerous pubs, bars, and fine and not-so-fine restaurants, a place where everybody meets for fun and entertainment. In the autumn of 1963, this was the site of my new job for three months before I had to spend some more time in the army.

Zunfthauses are busy places that provide catering services for weddings and social events. It wasn't an easy place to work. The kitchen was very small for the volume of food we put out, and we always worked long hours into the night, after which I had to walk quite a distance to my room on Beethoven Street. The first week I worked there wasn't too pleasant; I had to share a single room with eight rowdy Eastern Europeans. I was more than happy to get out of that environment.

My friend Geri Stocker, with whom I had spent time in the military in Losone, also happened to work in Zurich at the time. He was more than happy to hang out with me sometimes. One late November night Geri and I stopped at the Aelpli Bar, a well-known cozy bar that offered sing-along folk music, Swiss cheese specialties, fine adult beverages, and lots of conversation. That night, the usual noise at this place stopped abruptly as the latest news bulletin streamed over the airwaves of Swiss Radio. The speakers were turned up and we learned with horror of the assassination of JFK in Dallas. You could have heard a pin drop in the bar that night.

An unpleasant incident happened to me in Zurich late one Saturday night. I was finally getting off after a long day of work at the restaurant when I noticed an army of police vehicles sealing off part of the Niederdorf. It was a police raid, and everyone in the sealed area was arrested. I was arrested too. I happened to be in the wrong place at the wrong time. Luckily, the cops released me quickly after they had inspected my credentials. As I learned later, the cops tried to round up unregistered foreigners in the city.

I had to leave Zurich in late January of 1964 for military duty, and then back to Bürgenstock for the summer. Restaurant de la Tour in Lucerne was the perfect place for me in late summer of 1964, after the hotels closed. It was convenient and comfortable to stay at my parents' house before I move to St. Moritz for the coming winter. I had signed up for a winter season in the renowned Suvretta House in St. Moritz.

After the excitement of resort hotels, where something unexpected is always happening, a job in a small place like the Restaurant de la Tour can be quite boring, and this job was. The chef of this establishment was a good professional and a very polite man, and we worked well together. But the owner was very strange. He had been a chef himself at one time, but I never saw him in a good mood. He seemed very unapproachable and was never friendly. I soon found out about his temper, because I had to prepare lunch for him and his wife, who had a lifeless look on her face. One day as he sat down for their meal, he checked the temperature of the grilled tomatoes on his plate and decided that they were not hot enough. He got up from his table to pay me a visit behind the line in the kitchen. He grabbed the tomato from his plate, but luckily, I ducked in time. The tomato hit the wall behind me next to our pot washer Gaetano, a true Sicilian. I noticed the vendetta look on his face; he thought he was the target. The owner apologized later, but not before he chewed me out about that lukewarm tomato.

On one of my days off, I decided to see a movie at a cinema in the old part of the city. Before I had the chance to get to the ticket counter, a well-dressed, attractive lady stopped me and convinced me not to buy a ticket; she had an extra one that she had gotten from her employer and didn't want to waste it. If there is such a thing as love at first sight, this was it for both of us. After the show we went to a small bistro next door for a quick bite, and we talked for a long time. Hanni was married and had a two-year-old daughter, but she was going through a divorce. We left the eatery, kissed each other goodbye, and went our separate ways. She promised to visit me at the restaurant the next day by five in the evening. She was very punctual, and we had another date. From that moment on we were inseparable, and two years later we were engaged. She had a favorite dish called Entrecote Café de Paris. Soon I started to compose a version of Café Butter for her favorite dish. Mid-December came around quickly; I packed my few belongings and my tools and was on my way to St Moritz.

Anyone who hears the name St. Moritz will immediately think of a paradise for winter sports, a place illuminated in glamour. Yet its healing sources are far older than those in any other summer or winter resort. The healing waters of St. Moritz date back 3,000 years and are held in high esteem. In 1573, the therapeutic effect of this highly carbonated water was recorded by the Swiss German physician Paracelsus. As a result, St. Moritz became a renowned spa, and the small farming village of Engadin grew into a small town. Growth and development proceeded at a fast pace. In the twentieth century, new hotels were built at an astonishing rate. The fame of the resort grew when it hosted two Winter Olympiads, in 1928 and in 1948.

By mid-century, the wealthy were coming to St. Moritz to see and be seen. Aga Khan, King Faruk, King Feisal, Alfred Hitchcock, Richard Strauss, Charlie Chaplin, Enrico Caruso, the shah of Persia, Evita Peron, and many more luminaries traveled winter after winter to the picturesque town some 6,000 feet above sea level. During my short season at the Suvretta in 1964, Greek shipping tycoon Stavros Niarchos and Italian automaker Andrea Pininfarina occupied the best floors and suites. It was "the year of the alps" and the year of the Bobsleigh World Cup on the Cresta Run in St. Moritz.

A few years earlier, when I was still in culinary school, I had heard an incredible story about the Suvretta from an older gentleman who was sitting at the Stammtisch of a restaurant in Lucerne that my father and brother visited some evenings after work. A Stammtisch in most restaurants is a large table where locals love to meet and mostly talk about themselves, politics, and rumors. Conversations at the Stammtisch occasionally get quite heated. This old gent claimed that he had been the concierge at the Suvretta many years ago, probably in the golden twenties. He told us that an English lord traveled every winter for the whole month of February to the Suvretta and always requested the same suite in one of the towers of the hotel. But one year an Italian guest showed up and requested the exact same suite for the whole winter season. The concierge tried to explain to the Italian that this particular suite was reserved for the British lord and that he was expected to arrive in a week. The Italian was not impressed with the answer. He handed out a huge gratuity and demanded the suite at once, and he got it. The storyteller said: "Well, we sent a telegram to the English man, warning him to better remain in London for the winter, since there was an outbreak of cholera in St. Moritz!" Imagine this happening today with CNN and the Internet! The Englishman stayed in London that year, but he returned the following winter and rewarded them with a large gratuity and thanked them for the early warning that saved his life. Who knows whether the story is true, but it's a good one.

Suvretta House, St. Moritz

I arrived in St. Moritz in mid-December 1964. The train ride from Lucerne had taken more than five hours. I had to hire a taxi to get to the hotel, which is located some three kilometers outside St. Moritz in the small community of Campfer. I was quite nervous as I stood in front of the magnificent hotel, searching for the employee entrance. I had to ask a doorman for directions. The human resources office was tiny, and the young lady at the counter seemed to be quite busy. I tried to get her attention by explaining that I had been hired as one of the cooks. She asked for my name but then was distracted with a phone call. I received attention only when a tall, well-dressed gentleman showed up and greeted me with a smile. He introduced himself as the general manager. That certainly helped, and I overheard him say to the receptionist that she needed to be courteous to new employee arrivals. I was led by another employee to a service elevator near the kitchen. This gave me a good opportunity for a quick peek into the kitchen. Nervously I observed the chefs running all over the place. The hotel had opened that day and the stress of preparing for Christmas and New Year's had begun. A full house was anticipated. The smell of food made me hungry, since I hadn't eaten since early that morning, before my long train ride.

The elevator stopped at the top floor and then we walked to the end of the long hallway. My room was small, with only a bed, a small sink, a chair, a small wooden table, and an armoire. To my surprise, there was a telephone on my nightstand. Toilet and bath facilities were down the hall and were shared with other employees. I was asked to unpack and then return to the office.

After I was processed at the human resources office, I was finally escorted to the kitchen to meet Chef Hartley Mathis and the other chefs who were already on duty. Hartley Mathis was an impressive man with lots of energy. He was glad to see me and greeted me by saying "Oh, here we have the Bürgenstock fellow." His handshake was firm. My first impression was that he had a friendly demeanor, but because I knew that he was a star chef, my sense told me never to kid with that guy!

My new assignment was *chef de nuit*, night chef, which meant that I had to be there until the bar closed. That could well mean until 4 or 5 in the morning. Chef Mathis explained my schedule and my duties: "You need to be here at 10:30 in the morning and will be assigned wherever help is most needed. By 2:30 in the afternoon, you will be assigned afternoon duties from the *chef de parties*. It is very important," he continued, "that all their requests be met when they return at 5 p.m. for dinner service. Then you are in charge of having supper ready for 45 chefs at exactly 5 p.m., so they can sit down and have their dinner for half an hour. This has to be done exactly on time." I realized right away that it would be a difficult task to satisfy that many chefs day after day. Chef Mathis must have noticed my unease, because with a boyish grin on his face he explained, "If the food is good, you'll have a lot of friends here. Don't go overboard, just feed us well. After dinner, you take your break. You return by 8 p.m. and again help out where we need you, and after hours you will be responsible for all bar foods. The bar manager, Mario, will tell you when you can close the kitchen."

Chef also made it clear that on occasion I needed to be ready to come to work earlier if I was needed. That was why the phone was by my bed, so they could call me in early! I began to realize that I probably would be on standby most of the winter. Chef Mathis handed me a small booklet and asked me to log all the times I was on duty and to record all the orders for caviar and other high-priced food I got from the bar. He finished my orientation with "That's it, you start tomorrow at 10:30, see me if you have any questions."

I checked out the kitchen, where I saw two stoves, one large main stove for the guest service and a smaller one that was used by the cafeteria cooks, who prepared meals for some 400 employees. At night it was the service site for the grill room and restaurant, which had a sophisticated and rather complicated a la carte menu. Back in my room, I laid down for a while, a bit fearful and anxious about my new job. Cooking dinner for 45 professional chefs! Every day! It definitely weighed on my mind. At 5 p.m. I joined the chef's table with an army of cooks who were getting ready for dinner service. Chef Mathis introduced me to all my co-workers. My biggest worry at that moment was what I should prepare for all of them the next night.

The following morning, I showed up in the kitchen at 10 a.m. After lunch at 10:30, everyone switched into high gear for lunch service and I was told by Sous Chef Johnny Ehrat to help in the *garde manger*. It was a cold place, maybe 45 degrees Fahrenheit. I was assigned to some odd jobs while I listened to the powerful voice of Chef Mathis announcing incoming meals in French. This information was transmitted through loud speakers everywhere. The butcher was prepping and cutting meats for upcoming menus. Some of the local cooks spoke Romansh, the native language of St Moritz. I didn't understand a word of it. Most of the guys had been on the job for one or two days, just like me, and most likely they were just as nervous as I was. Lunch service was over between 2 and 2:30 p.m., and everyone went on their break until 5 p.m. At that point, the stove was turned off and I received my specific duties for the afternoon.

Everyone had something for me to do. Straining the consommé, blanching the dinner vegetables, straining the demiglaze and reducing it by half, then putting on a fresh grand jus. Placing the sole filets in buttered *sautoirs* with finely chopped shallots for one of the dinner's first courses. The *rôtisseurs* reminded me to turn the electric grill on high by exactly 4 p.m. Then I had to prepare 15 gallons of fresh iced tea for the chefs. The cafeteria chefs asked me to griddle ratatouille for the employee's dinner menu, and of course I wasn't to forget to turn on the oil stove by 4 p.m.! In addition, I had to prepare the occasional bar menu orders of smoked salmon, beef tartar, etc. The list went on and on.

But when was I going to have time to prepare the chefs' dinner that had to be ready at 5 p.m.? My little notebook was full of requests and I was plenty stressed and afraid that I wouldn't be able to complete everything in time. This was the season when I learned time management! I do remember the dinner I delivered for the 45 chefs that first night. I knew it had to be perfect. I had dreamed about it half the night. The other half, I couldn't sleep. I prepared sautéed pork chops with a port wine sauce that I stole from the *saucier*, spaghetti Napolitaine, a nice mixed seasonal salad with house vinaigrette, and of course the obligatory iced tea.

Everything was set by 5p.m., but admittedly, I struggled. The butcher wanted to know if I had taken his precut pork chops from the cooler. I had, and he wasn't happy with my answer.

Chef Mathis didn't care about the meal, since he followed a diet most of the season that consisted of tangerines and a pot of hot tea. But I felt everyone else's tense anticipation that night. I sat down for dinner too, but I no longer had any appetite. Every request I had written down in my little book was scratched off and no one had complained about my work, except for the *rôtisseurs*, who said that the grill had not been hot enough.

I had survived the first half of my first day. I went up to my lonely room for my evening break. I took a hot shower; I smelled of sole filets, ratatouille, and demiglaze. At 8 p.m., as I walked toward the kitchen from the service elevator, Chef Mathis, who was standing at the counter, spotted me and hollered "Peyer! Get with the *rôtisseurs*." Dinner service was at its height. I reported to the two local St. Moritz fellows who were helplessly in the weeds with the evening's entrée, *entrecôte double*. Most of the guests ordered this menu choice that night, and almost all the sirloins were undercooked. Instead of being *a point*, or medium rare, the meat was served *bleu*, which means basically raw. Mathis had a total fit, and some of the fire-proofed *cocottes* that the meat was presented in went flying back to the stove and shattered in a hundred pieces. It was intimidating, and I asked myself if this would be an everyday routine. The grill really wasn't hot enough, and each time we put new steaks on, it cooled down even more. The guys gave me funny looks when I put a dozen or so *entrecôtes double* on the stainless-steel edge of the hot stove, a trick I had learned during my apprenticeship. It speeded up the process, and the steaks cooked twice as fast. "Screw that grill," I mumbled, "you guys need a new one and don't blame me for it anymore." Unfortunately, it was too late; the numerous complaints had made Chef Mathis red faced and visibly angry. The *rôtisseurs* thanked me for my help, I gained some instant credibility, and my confidence level went up a notch after this first day of work.

Dinner service was over, but my day was not. Now my first night shift started, and I had absolutely no clue about what to expect. Everyone was gone by 10 p.m. with the exception of the chef, the *sous chef*, and the pastry chef. The *rôtisserie* guys left for the night after they received a serious butt-kicking in the chef's office for the undercooked beef they had served all night. My first task was to make 70 to 80 sandwiches for various night-shift employees. In addition, the department heads had special requests; these included the night concierge; the entertainment director, or *chef de plaisir*, as he was titled; and a few more managerial staffers. Edna, a beautiful and very attractive vocalist from the Italian show band, came into the kitchen and introduced herself. I promised her quickly that I would take good care of her; she was truly charming. Five minutes later the guys from the band showed up and introduced themselves. The bar manager, Mario, turned out to be a wonderful guy to work with. He communicated well and was a lot of fun. I realized that these were all hardworking people who spent night after night doing their jobs and in many cases did not have a single day off during the entire season. They deserved a meal of their choice.

At 3:30 a.m., Mario paid a quick visit to the kitchen to inform me that bar activities were over, and my first workday ended. I marked my time in the booklet Chef Mathis had given me, closed the kitchen, and went up to my top-floor room. It took me a while to get used to such unusual hours. We had no *saucier* for the winter season; the one the hotel had hired had not shown up. Hartley Mathis was a bit nervous because this important position was not filled. A German named Wolfgang Sauer who actually was the *tournant* was filling the gap for the time being. Wolfgang was a great guy with plenty of personality. But then Chef Mathis hired a Frenchman whom everybody spoke of as a superstar. The chef was very happy when this Gilbert Bécaud lookalike arrived for his debut. I felt sorry for the Frenchman; we realized immediately that in no way he could keep up with the fast pace of the hotel kitchen. He lasted three days, after which he packed his belongings and returned to France. After that our friend Wolfgang got the promotion to *chef saucier*, which we all were happy about, as he deserved it.

I cannot remember how many gala dinners we had that particular winter, but I will never forget the intensity and organized confusion of those long nights. The menus were very French and its presentations very nice. On gala dinner nights, I had to return to the kitchen at 9:30 p.m, since the dinner service started very late. I was lucky to be finished by 6 a.m. On one gala night, I waited for more than ten minutes in the hallway of the floor where I lived for the service elevator instead of taking the stairs. I was ten minutes late to work, and I promptly received an emotional outburst from Chef Mathis. It was loud and clear, and I needed a couple of hours to digest it. In typical Mathis fashion, he called me to his office after gala service and handed me a beer, saying "You are a nice fellow, Peyer." I knew this was his apology for screaming at me.

Usually Chef Mathis assigned me to Wolfgang to help him expedite two or three of the fancy entrées. The grill room and restaurant were always sold out, and I was often assigned to work there as well. Our excellent restaurateur chef, Vincent Bosotto, had to do a gold medal performance with our a la carte and "a la minute" menu. (Vincent later became the team chef of the Swiss Culinary Olympics team.) Food was delivered to our wait staff from two counters. On counter #1 was Chef Mathis with the microphone and a huge mirror mounted above. Without turning he could follow all the activities in the kitchen and follow our movements and see our reactions. Each order he hollered through his microphone had to be answered with a "Oui, Chef." If you did not answer, you were screamed at. It was a noisy environment. Counter #2, which was designated for the grill room and restaurant, was run by Sous Chef Johnny Ehrat. He did not call out the orders; he just checked the outgoing dishes for quality and proper presentation. Chef Mathis called all orders and was always in the weeds when it started to get hectic. One time he stopped the dining-room gala service for a moment and started reading all the a la carte orders at once, which created massive confusion. Poor Vincent had to answer with a "Oui Chef" for each order! I never understood that system. Sous Chef Ehrat could have easily handled the grill room and restaurant by himself without all that cross-hollering. My guess is that Chef Mathis wanted to have control over everything.

By 11:30 or midnight, gala service would be over and the exhausted chefs would be rewarded with a beer or two. Their night was over, but mine was just starting. One time Maitre Rossier, the polished *maitre d'hotel* who was a native of Geneva, came to the kitchen and asked for a wonderful dinner for the 73 waiters and waitresses for that night's gala. He expected to have the meal served by 3 a.m., after everything was cleaned up and the dining room was set for following day's breakfast. With the blessings of Chef Mathis, I was able to serve them their favorite rump steak, French fries, salads, and a variety of desserts prepared by the pastry chefs. By the time this small banquet was served, Edna and the boys in the band also wanted to have their gala feast.

I did not have half a day off until late January, which meant I worked four hours in the morning and had the evening off. It felt like going on an extended vacation. During my three-month stay in St. Moritz, I was scheduled for three days off in all. You can imagine how I appreciated and enjoyed them!

The demanding pace of work must have created an urgent need for Vitamin C for all of us. One of the six reach-in refrigerators in our *garde manger* was stocked with delicious Birds Eye frozen fruit juices, including boysenberry, blackberry, orange, blood orange, and other varieties. The cooks, *commis*, and apprentices who worked past 10:30 p.m. would wait until the chef and the *garde manger* chef left for the evening, and then raids the reach-in for the juices. What we did not know was that one night Chef Mathis was watching. From his position outside in the dark parking lot, he could see into the well-lit *garde manger* very well. Obviously someone had tipped him off. He wrote down all the names of the "juice violators," and I happened to be one of them. I just loved those juices. At the chef's table the following day at lunch, when everyone was present, Chef Mathis called out names, including mine, of course. We had to stand up in front of everybody. It was embarrassing. "These are the fine guys," the chef announced, "who are drinking our fruit juices empty after hours. I also said a prayer that you will all get diarrhea from drinking the stuff." He proceeded to the punishment phase: "The apprentices will do a whole night shift and shape 300 pounds of chateau potatoes, and you, Peyer, will supervise them and make sure it's done." It was very awkward standing there with all the other chefs laughing at us. They enjoyed those juices too, I knew, but they had not been caught. It was a long night shaping these Chateau potatoes. We finished when Mathis started his day at 7 a.m.

Chef's Christmas Party at the Suvretta

My next surprise came only a couple of weeks after the juice debacle. Mathis came looking for me and asked me to follow him to the general manager's office. That really did not sound good. I had no idea why or what to expect. I felt the accelerated pounding of my heart as I followed the chef. "What has happened?" I asked Mathis with a jittery voice as we walked through the hotel lobby. He did not reply, and his silence made it worse. As we walked up the stairs from the lobby to the general manager's office, I desperately tried to think of anything I could have done wrong. The general manager was not smiling when we entered his domain, a stark contrast from his friendly welcome the day I arrived in St. Moritz. "It was reported to me," he began, "that you let three or four chefs prepare themselves large *entrecôtes* at three o'clock in the morning after they returned to the hotel from a night out drinking in town. All of them were intoxicated, according to our source, and you, Mr. Peyer, provided the steaks for their early morning treat. You are the night chef, aren't you?" He pointed his finger at me and explained that this meant a written reprimand and a 100-franc deduction from my next paycheck to cover the hotel's expenses.

I was stunned and upset. Chef Mathis looked angrily at me, and I was afraid that any minute he was going to rip my head off. It was time to defend myself. I had the courage to interrupt and ask the date of the incident. I knew with confidence that I had absolutely nothing to do with this matter. It had happened some two weeks earlier. Why had they waited so long to confront me? Luckily, it quickly became apparent that I was not the guilty one, as the date of the incident was checked against my schedule. It was that first evening off! "Do you know who was working that night?" the general manager asked. Chef and I knew, since the same fellow chef had replaced me for each of my three evenings off during the season. We left the office, Mathis still angry. My guess was that he wanted to know the names of the chefs who had indulged themselves with the prime beef; the incident report did not mention the names of the culprits. Our night concierge, who reported it, did not recognize our colleagues. Returning to the kitchens, I went to look for Erwin Osterwalder, who had replaced me on the night of the incident, but he already knew what was coming. Word traveled fast! I promised him that I would recover the money that would be deducted from his paycheck. "But you need to tell me the names of the culprits," I told him. The names were no surprise: Wolfgang Sauer, Andy Niggli the *rôtisseur*, the pastry chef, and Chef Donaz, all of them special darlings of Chef Mathis. The poor kid could not have stopped them because they were his bosses. The guys just helped themselves. They appeared to be as hungry as grizzly bears after consuming numerous adult beverages and walking uphill for almost two miles to the Suvretta in below-freezing temperatures. The night concierge had gotten upset when he saw the guys devouring juicy steaks and loaves of freshly baked French bread while he got a salami sandwich and a few chips for his dinner.

I talked to my colleagues the next day, and they all agreed to pay Osterwalder the 100 francs. Behind closed doors in Chef Mathis's office; the four late-night diners received a significant emotional experience. I would have loved to have witnessed that conversation. I saw all of them leave his office with their tails between their legs.

When March arrived, I knew that I would not be employed much longer. Our contractual agreement with the hotel gave it the right to give seven days notice for termination when the season came to an end. Business was slow. Some nights I could leave as early as 2 a.m. Mario, the bar manager, would call me if a food order came in. I started working earlier in the morning, mostly in the *garde manger*. One day during lunchtime we decided to entertain ourselves. A guy from Basel who we called Skinny was known as the kitchen clown. We told Skinny that we would pay him 25 francs if he would climb on top of the reach-in and jump into the trout tank, which was about three times the size of a bathtub. We knew that we weren't likely to be caught because this was the time when Chef Mathis was expediting over the microphone. We did not have to ask Skinny twice. He nodded and said, "Not a problem, I'll do it." We collected the money. I contributed 5 francs. One of the guys stayed near the hallway to warn us in case the chef decided to visit our *garde manger*. Skinny climbed on top of the reach-in, we removed the cover from the trout tank, and he jumped into the icy-cold water in full uniform. The impact threw at least a dozen trout out of the tank, and they were jumping all over the kitchen floor. It was a challenge to catch the slippery and bouncing fish and put them back into the tank. There were light snow flurries outside and it was very cold in the *garde manger*, something we had not thought through. Skinny was shaking cold and his wet uniform was sticking to his body. "If the chef gets wind of this, or God forgive us, if he comes back to our area, we'll have an early or immediate departure for sure," we said. One of the quicker-thinking guys ran down to the laundry and came back with three sets of sheets. We wrapped Skinny in the sheets, and his roommate carried him down to the laundry, which was right next to Skinny's room. They had to pass the chef's counter and we heard Mathis asking what was going on. Our colleague kept on walking by the counter and replied that he was just dropping off some dirty kitchen rags at the laundry. It was a good thing that Skinny was a very tiny person! Skinny returned 20 minutes later in a fresh uniform and 25 francs richer.

Soon enough our illustrious chef called a meeting at the chef's table with a list of the dates of our departures. We all listened with trepidation for our names to be called. Chef also had a list of immediately available interim jobs for us to choose from. There were numerous openings for an upcoming industrial fair in Basel. But when Mathis called my name and informed me that I would be terminated in one week, to my great surprise, he offered me the chance to stay another three weeks in St. Moritz at the renowned Villa Suvretta. I was very happy to replace the Villa's chef, who was going on a three-week vacation to his native Italy. Mathis told me that I would have to negotiate the salary with the Villa's manager.

The Villa is located in the wealthiest section of St. Moritz. On the Suvretta hill above St. Moritz, it is not enough to own just one glitzy home. Ideally, you should have two, and possibly three. The Agnellis have three, as do the Heinekens. The Niarchos families own two, the same as the Perfettis, the Italian confectionery family best known for Brooklyn Chewing Gum. The 47 huge homes built on Switzerland's most expensive piece of residential real estate belong to Europe's corporate elite. Often the only sign of habitation is a guard outside. Most of the residents receive more than enough publicity at home, and the Suvretta's privacy and discretion are its prize attributes. Here, "For Sale" signs look as inappropriate as a man from Mars.

The next day, on my way to visit the Villa to introduce myself, I noticed an older gentlemen sitting on the front porch of the Villa. He was wearing a Gamsbart hat and was busy looking at the surrounding mountains with his binoculars. Marcus, the Villa's *portier*, invited me in and introduced me to Mr. Gredig, the elderly gentlemen with the binoculars. Gredig is a common name in that part of Switzerland, and this man was no relation to the one who kicked my butt. He was a wonderful and friendly older man, and we quickly became involved in a great conversation. He told me that presently there were only two guests in the Villa. He gave me a quick tour of the magnificent place and then invited me back to his beloved porch for a cup of coffee. He asked if I liked to ski. "I really do," I answered, "but I never find time to do so." "I'll take care of that while you here," he replied as he watched everything through his binoculars. I was convinced that he was searching for some nice-looking ski bunnies on the nearby slopes. A very polite young Italian couple served us coffee. Without talking details, Mr. Gredig told me that he would pay me the same salary I had at the hotel. For an instant, I thought I had died and gone to heaven! I would receive my salary for doing basically nothing! His request for me to start the following day was quickly settled with Chef Mathis. Chef's typically direct and unceremonious response to me was "Okay, Peyer, get the hell out of here and best of luck to you."

My new living quarter was a luxurious guest room at the Villa that faced the hillside behind the building. I could not believe it at first. The scenery in the backyard was so beautiful with its lush evergreens and lawn still partly covered with snow. Many mornings when I opened the window to enjoy some of the fresh, still, and chilly mountain air, I saw a couple of red deer making their rounds. I felt pampered; Marcus would knock on my door every morning at seven with a pot of fresh aromatic coffee for me. That was unusual, and I started to wonder why he was doing that. He also wanted to shine my work shoes every day. When I told him that that was unnecessary, he replied, "That's okay; we all really love to have you here." It took me a few days to get used to this unusual treatment, and I soon learned the reason behind it. The vacationing chef obviously was a tyrant who demanded this kind of service, and I sensed that the few employees at the Villa were afraid of him.

On my first day at work at the Villa I prepared a menu for our two guests in a small but workable kitchen. By eleven o'clock I had served lunch for the six or seven employees. They could not believe they were getting the same food as the guests and were convinced that I had made a mistake. I sat down and ate lunch with them and tried to make them understand that there would not be a separate menu for the employees. When they told me what the chef usually served them, I got the picture. They really were working in an unpleasant environment. They got leftover food, while the chef helped himself to the guest menu. Did Gredig know about it? My assumption was that he did not. He lived somewhere else and never got directly involved in the operation of the Villa. I concluded that the chef was the boss and that he chose to treat his people like dirt. Some of the stories told are not suitable to be repeated in this book. What a shame, I thought. I knew that these nice folks were not looking forward to the chef's return from Italy. I finally convinced Marcus to stop bringing coffee in the morning, knowing he would have to resume this service again after I left. It was such a drastic change from the hotel to the villa; I could not find enough things to do. It was more of a vacation than a job. Some days we didn't have any guests. On those days, Mr. Gredig would send me to the ski slopes at his expense. The skiing there was best. Thanks to Gredig I was able to ski Corviglia, Diavolezza, and Lagalp. All paid for! He had a drawer full of cable-cart and ski-lift tickets to give away. What a benefit that was. The three weeks passed quickly. In early April it was time to say good-bye to the very small group of truly wonderful people at the Villa Suvretta. I wished I could have stayed another three weeks. Marcus drove me to the train station, and I left St. Moritz for my hometown of Lucerne.

My experience at Davos for six weeks during the months of January and February 1966 was extraordinary and by any measure far from usual business. After I was summoned into the army again in the late autumn 1965, there was little or no chance that I could get full-time seasonal employment for the coming winter. Early in January, as I was looking for something temporary in my hometown, I ran into my old boss, Chef Rüegsegger, which turned out to be a blessing. He had been asked by the Gredig family at the Fluela Hotel to find a qualified individual to replace one of their chefs, who had suffered a severe injury on the job. Very happy about this temporary employment, I arrived in Davos two days later. There was no World Economic Forum in the sixties, but the city of Davos hosted the World Figure Skating Championship that season. I got off the train directly across from the Fluela Hotel, checked myself in, and visited the kitchen at once to introduce myself. Mr. Schmidt, the executive chef, assigned me to the *rôtisseur's* position. The crew was already there and the season was in full swing. Starting on a busy day and not knowing anybody among the staff made me anxious. I am certain that I had one of my scary pre-first-day dreams the night before, but this time the dream became reality! With plenty of uneasiness, I started my temporary assignment at a fully occupied hotel.

One of the menu items the second or third day on the job was quiche, designed for our quick lunch menu at the small Stübli restaurant, which usually offered a reasonably priced and fast luncheon for the numerous skiers taking a midday break. Chef Schmidt was kind enough to hand me his own special recipe for quiche, reminding me to pay attention to it. I went to work, starting on the batter, which I then handed over to our pastry chef, whose duty it was to pour it into the quiche pans lined with the rolled-out dough. When the quiche was baked, he would deliver it back to my station and I would service the individual orders for the restaurant. Very easy! Not a problem.

But by 10:30 that morning, the pastry chef approached me to tell me that we had a small problem. He didn't even know my name yet. He tried to be very polite and explained that the quiche wouldn't bake, it just would not rise. I checked the quiche and he was right; it really looked as if it had been eaten once before! Holy shit! I had forgotten to add the eggs to the batter! And the restaurant would open at 11:30 for business, a scary experience on my second day on the job. The pastry chef had to dump all ten of the quiches, then roll out fresh dough again and I went to work with high speed on a new batter, this time with eggs in it. We made it in time and gave each other a high five. I was relieved; the quiche was delicious and the chef never found out what happened.

Chef Schmidt had a full beard and at times seemed a bit strange. He loved to talk about himself, always pointing out what a great chef he was. He always found fault with the sauces, and his judgments were very arbitrary. I was the one who had to prepare all the sauces, and I found myself at the receiving end of his criticism. He demanded that he taste and critique all of the sauces before anything could leave the kitchen. Every day, I had to take each of the sauces to his office on a small saucer with a mocha spoon. After slurping the various sauces from the spoons, he always had the same answer: "Give it another half a turn from the peppermill and a hint of salt!" After the correction was done, I had to do the whole spiel again. Chef Schmidt then had the same arbitrary and routine answer: "See Eduard, I told you so! Now it's a perfect sauce." After a few weeks on the job, I decided to do a test on the chef. After I brought him a port wine sauce for his approval and had gotten the now-very-repetitious reply of peppermill and salt, I went back to my station and made sure that he was not watching me. I then returned to his office with the exact same sauce. Chef Schmidt's reply: "See Eduard, I told you so! Now it's a perfect sauce."

The day our injured colleague was released from the doctor's care and returned to work came rather quickly, which meant that I had to go. Hanni showed up for a two-day visit and to drive me home, believing that I was done in Davos, as did I. But there was more work for me just around the corner. The World Figure Skating Championship in Davos was shortly to end, and the Soviets were favored to dominate the event as usual. The closing ceremonies for 1,200 guests were scheduled to take place at the Grand Hotel Belvedere, the largest hotel in Davos. The day after my release from the Fluela Hotel, I was hired at the Belvedere for the duration of the championship. Chef Schmidt had arranged it. He had received a SOS call from the human resources office at the Belvedere. Hanni dropped me off at the Grand Hotel and returned to Lucerne without me. Mr. Tanno, the hotel's general manager, offered me compensation of 70 francs per day. That was a very good salary at the time. I even met two old friends from Lucerne, Marcus and Hans, who were brothers. Hans was the *saucier* and Marcus managed the *garde manger*. I started the job the same day, but I could never have imagined what was to come. The hotel was fully occupied, which meant some 350 breakfasts, luncheons, and dinners. There was no time during the day to work on all the showpieces, ice carvings, and butter sculptures needed for the gala, so this work was scheduled for after hours. Our schedules for the next two weeks were merciless and brutal. We ate breakfast at 7:30 a.m., followed by regular preparation and the usual business of the day until 10:30 a.m., when we ate our lunch. This was followed by lunch service for hotel guests at 2:30 p.m., after which we had a break of an hour and a half. At 4 p.m. we met with the executive chef to discuss the job assignments for the night shift. At

5 p.m., there a short half-hour dinner for the crew, followed by dinner service for the hotel guests. At 9:30 p.m., we had a one-hour break. At 10:30 p.m., we received our assignments for the preparations for that night for the closing ceremony gala. At 4:00 a.m., dinner for all the chefs working on the gala event, which was usually a big steak, a salad, and a beverage of choice. There was one exception. The employees' cook, a young German fellow, enjoyed a regular schedule; after all, someone had to prepare the meals for all the employees. We all disliked him because of that.

The first few days were somehow manageable; at least we got a little sleep. But after five or six days we began to feel the impact of this grueling schedule. Fatigue began to set in. Our chef's temper began to get out of line, some of us started to oversleep in the morning, and everything began to slow down. Many overslept during the short afternoon break or dozed off during the 4 p.m. meeting with the chef. No one was all there! Dinner service began to deteriorate because of severe fatigue, and more accidents occurred, such as cuts and burns. Fatigue turned into exhaustion and with that, bad things began to happen. An early morning gunshot right at the front door of our sleeping quarters made us all sit up straight in our beds. It took me a while to realize what was going on, and then we heard a commotion in the hallway. We all came out of our rooms and saw the chef wearing his pajamas beating the living daylight out of the German employees' cook, who was already bloody and lying on the floor in a fetal position. We had to come to his rescue and stopped the chef before he killed our helpless colleague. He had come home at 5 a.m. after consuming too many beers and Steinhäger shooters and thought he would do us a favor by firing a blank gun to wake us up for another day of work. Most of us had just gone to bed and were in a deep and sound sleep. I never found out what happened to the chef, but the German was terminated, which was maybe a good thing, since the chef would have terminated him in his own way!

That was only the beginning. The following night the chef again had a rather loud argument, this time with one of the waiters, who called him an asshole. That did not go over well, and it ended in a rather nasty and bloody fistfight in the middle of the kitchen and in front of everyone.

We had to do several ice sculptures for the event. Back in those days, there were no companies to call who could deliver a block of ice or ice carving companies who could deliver the finished product. We had to travel one afternoon to the nearby Davoser Lake with ice picks and saws and carve a dozen blocks out of the frozen lake!

Finally the day of the closing ceremonies arrived. My roommate, the pastry chef, was very exhausted, and so was I. We had our doubts about whether we could make it through the day. The weather was gorgeous outside; deep blue skies, lots of sunshine, and enormous amounts of fresh snow, which had fallen for two or three days. The function we had to orchestrate was so important, and I knew that it would be my last day at the hotel. We schlepped ourselves down to the kitchens. We noticed Mr. Morosani, the owner of the Belvedere, making his rounds, accompanied by Tanno, our general manager, and a third individual with an attaché case. He was a physician whom Morosani had hired to give us all some kind of booster shot to get us through that last day. We dropped our pants in the *garde manger* and received an injection, only God knows what, in our butts, while Morosani and Tanno praised us for the wonderful job we were performing for the Grand Hotel.

It kept us awake for a while longer, that was all. Our executive chef looked bad, very bad. The pressures he endured must have been overwhelming. We still were slaving away past midnight as the event slowly came to an end. It was a great function indeed, and I recall the unruly behavior of the Soviets, who won most of the gold medals that year. That was the year of Ludmila Belousova and Oleg Protopopov. The vodka was flowing steadily all night. I slept until the next afternoon, got up and packed my belongings, went to see the chef and my co-workers to say good-bye, and ate dinner with the crew at 5 p.m. Then I went out of the hotel the first time in weeks for some drinks. It felt great. The following morning, ready to leave Davos, I knocked on the general manager's office door. "Come on in!" Tanno shouted. "Eduard! You survived it." He stood up from behind his desk and shook my hand. "Thank you very much for your help; that wasn't easy for any of us," he said. "We appreciate that you were able to help us out." He asked me to sit down. Tanno swiveled his chair around to face the safe on the wall. He looked back at me and asked, "What did we say we would pay you?" "70 francs," I replied. "Correct," he murmured as he opened the safe. He grabbed a bundle of cash and started counting. He turned toward me and told me that he and Mr. Morosani had decided to double my pay. "It's quite all right; we really appreciated your efforts. Have fun with the extra cash and have a nice trip home." I was totally speechless; I had never expected such generous treatment! I left Davos very happy and thought to myself that effort pays off, hoping that it would stay like that. I never found out what happened to our temperamental chef with regard to his numerous confrontations with employees, but then, I did not care anymore. It was time for some leisure, and for the next two weeks, I enjoyed great times in Amsterdam, The Hague, and Rotterdam visiting friends from Indonesia and Holland whom I had worked with in St. Moritz.

In 1967, I spent my last summer in Switzerland, once again at the Bellevue in Engelberg, the place of my apprenticeship. That summer gave me some time to plan for the future. Chef Rubis offered me the position of *saucier, sous chef*, with the exception that I was paid more than the 50 francs I received during my last season of education. It gave me a great opportunity to gain more experience, but being around the same folks again was not very enlightening. Ruth was still drunk at least three times a week, and Frau Susie still wanted that ridiculous Kaiserschmarrn. Nothing really was that different, except that I enjoyed a nice room at the villa next door, the place where Dr. Odermatt and his wife Ruth lived. A knock on my door late one night woke me up from a deep sleep. I put my chef's pants on and opened the door. Ruth walked straight into my room with very few clothes on and a cigarette in her mouth, asking for a match. I must say, she still had the body of a model. I could smell the booze; she was tanked! Then the loud voice came from her husband's upstairs bedroom, asking "Where are you?" It gave me a chill; all I needed was Dr. Odermatt coming down the stairs and seeing me with only chef's pants on with his half-naked wife in my room! Sitting on my bed! I knew he had a sizeable gun collection upstairs. Ruth left quickly, after her husband hollered for her once more. The following morning, I had to tell the story to Chef Rubis. He told me, "Eddie that is the reason I live in the hotel now. The exact same thing happened to me on several occasions when I used to live in the same room as you do now."

As autumn approached, I left Engelberg for good. Newspaper advertising in the late summer of 1967 for a new "Swiss Center" in London had caught my interest, and I applied for a job there. It was to be operated by the popular Swiss restaurant chain Mövenpick. I traveled to Zurich with great enthusiasm when I received the call for an interview. The job screening went well and I had the opportunity to meet the chefs and management involved in the London project. I was required to work at the Zurich property for at least three months and then relocate to London. My job was interesting that second time around in Zurich; I worked in a modern, well-organized restaurant operation, although it was top heavy in management. I benefited professionally from their creative seasonal promotions and the well-organized off-premise catering business. We had some fun too, when the pastry chef and I made a new apprentice run all over Zurich in search of a soufflé pump after telling him that we had misplaced ours. The poor guy had a really unpleasant experience as he tried to get that soufflé pump at three or four different franchises of our chain. We were caught in the act by Chef Mundrich and had a very unpleasant experience at his office. We were asked to apologize to the victim in front of him, and we did. I must have worked too long with Tony Peter, I mumbled. The three months went by quickly. The desire to go to London passed as well. Meager pay and the high cost of living in England changed my mind. Still, I had a strong desire to get away from the seasonal jobs, and I searched for other opportunities away from Switzerland. My profession and my skills were in big demand at the time. Hanni, now my fiancée went to the University of Bern and began a semester of medical school, then planned to move to Basel to open a cosmetic and foot massage business. She needed some medical education for the business she was planning. Our once-passionate relationship began to cool off some as we both searched for professional opportunities and started to drift farther apart.

Back home in Lucerne, I learned from my mother that her brother was visiting from the United States. I hardly remembered him; I must have been around six or seven years old when Uncle Max last visited us in Switzerland. In the meantime, I signed a nonbinding agreement with Sheraton in Panama City, Panama. As I was trying to obtain a visa to Panama, Uncle Max arrived in Switzerland. His visit began to change everything! He persuaded me not to go to Panama, and today I am thankful for that. Max had some other big plans for the two of us. He spent over three months in Switzerland and told me about a great location in Pennsylvania and an opportunity for us to operate a restaurant in a small hotel on the shores of the Delaware River. He sponsored me, and within a month I had a visa for legal entry to the United States from the U.S. Consulate in Zurich.

Max started to spend money on kitchen equipment like a drunken sailor. Our plan was to open a small place with cheese and other Swiss specialties. It sounded very exiting! I pictured a lovely small inn on the Delaware River with Max running the front and me cooking up a storm in the kitchen. Max had been a maitre d' in renowned Swiss resorts before he emigrated to the United States. At over 70 years old he was still entrepreneurial and full of great ideas. By January 1968 he had shipped all the equipment to the United States to be stored; it looked like a full metric ton. Max was serious! At the end of February 1968, the family gathered at the Zurich-Kloten Airport. The day had arrived for our departure. My parents were happy and sad at the same time. We were drinking some coffee at a standup counter before we went to the gates. Unexpectedly and out from nowhere, Hanni stood in front of us; she had traveled from Basel to the airport in Zurich to say good-bye. It was emotional and not without tears, and it was very evident that we still missed each other very much.

4. Putting Down Roots in the United States

Uncle Max and I boarded a Swissair DC-8, departing for New York. The day we touched down at Kennedy Airport was chilly and windy. We stood in line for some time, but finally made it through immigration. Max wanted to go to the place where all of his shipped equipment was stored; I remember it was somewhere in New Jersey. We traveled by bus, and I had no clue where we were. It was dark as we stepped out of that bus in the small town of Lumberville, Pennsylvania, around 8:30 p.m. The motel was located on a country road, not on a highway as Max had always described it to me. It looked ordinary and plain to me. The small motel was located directly on the Delaware River. We could see the lights of Trenton, New Jersey across the water. We entered the very small lobby. The lights were mostly out; I don't believe there was a single guest on the property. What the hell is this, I wondered; it was so very different from what I had envisioned. A middle-aged couple came out of the office and greeted us warmly. Dorothy and Jeffrey Kessler were delightful people. They looked wealthy, and as I learned later, they were. He was a retired stockbroker from Wall Street who had wanted to move out of the city, so he had bought himself a small motel some 50 miles from New York City. We were tired after the long flight and bus ride, so we retired for the night in a comfortable room. When we got up at 9 a.m., we met the Kesslers in a tiny and plain-looking coffee shop on the premises. I was curious about where the dining room was. I was in it!

I was right; there wasn't a single guest in the house. Mrs. Kessler cooked some bacon and eggs for the four of us. We ate breakfast and talked. I spoke only a few words of English, so Max acted as my interpreter. The motel sat directly on the Delaware River. Next door was a very old building that almost looked like a haunted house called the Black Bass Hotel. There was a small general store directly across from our motel, then a few small houses, and that was it. "It's all yours; by the weekend you can expect a full house," Jeffrey Kessler assured us.

I was enthusiastic. Max and I went shopping to put a menu together for the upcoming weekend. I have a small kitchen in my present home in San Antonio, but the one at the motel was half its size, suitable for preparing only continental breakfasts. I started to wonder what I gotten myself into. But my drive to do something different returned quickly. Somehow we were going to make this thing work.

We purchased some other necessities from the general store across the street, which was owned by an impressive-looking retired marine sergeant. Friday evening came, and the Black Bass Hotel next door filled up with a bunch of rowdy folks. Its small restaurant and bar were packed. Our place with its 30 rooms started to sell out, too. Exciting, I thought. The small eating area started to look nice and comfortable. Max still knew what he was doing, he still had the touch. We had a record crowd of four diners for the evening! All couples, behaving quietly and like they were very much in love, while next door the loud and rowdy crowd continued to eat and drink into the wee hours of the morning. To make a long story short, all of the Kessler's guests were personal friends, stockbroker buddies who brought their mistresses and secretaries to rural New Jersey for an exciting weekend retreat. What a business plan. Now I knew why his clientele were not the slightest bit interested in culinary concoctions. Their minds were elsewhere.

Saturday night was not much different. By Sunday afternoon everyone had checked out and the place again stood empty and

Lumberville once again resembled a ghost town. There was absolutely nothing else to do, and I was quickly overcome with boredom. After eight or nine days in Lumberville and another failed weekend, even Max began to realize that this adventure was a faux pas. I worried about all his equipment in storage. Max was much more optimistic; he thought he might be able to sell it. I do not know if he ever did. The next day, Max's wife showed up. I had no idea that his home was a few miles down the river in Yardley, Pennsylvania. Just a day before Gertrude found us, Max confessed to me that he had run away from her because he wanted to do something different in his life. That is why he had traveled to his native Switzerland. I loved the man and felt sorry for him. We packed our belongings and moved to Yardley. I stayed at his home and actually started contemplating returning to Switzerland. Mrs. Kessler had tears in her eyes as we left the motel.

I had no job, no income! I wouldn't last long like that! I had many sleepless nights at Max's house, listening to the trains across the Delaware River in Trenton, New Jersey. Hanni was on my mind too; I was sure we would get together again. Good old Max started to drive me around in his old Plymouth from Yardley to New Hope to Allentown, trying to help me find a job. He must have felt bad about everything.

I remember stopping at a restaurant called Washington Crossing to talk to the chef about a job as a cook. He started to brag about how every single item in his kitchen was made from scratch. He said that his vichyssoise was the house specialty, while I counted at least four dozen #10 cans of that particular soup on one of his storeroom shelves. Then he asked me if I had an idea what a vichyssoise was. I was tempted to tell him to have closer a look at his shelf.

Max had a rather bad habit while he was driving; when he started a conversation with me; he always looked at me and forgot to pay attention to the road. Many times I tried to remind him to pay attention to the road, but Max kept on doing it. As we drove through Princeton one afternoon, he hit a concrete wall and his old

Plymouth was history! It was a blessing that we did not get hurt. As the New Jersey State Police arrived at the scene, I overheard Max telling them some story about a deer crossing the road. Without a car, the job search became an even more pressing issue. But things always work out, and I found employment at the local golf club in Yardley. For about four dollars per hour, I landed a broiler cook job and started to grill the rib eyes, strip sirloins, and, of course, the burgers. I was happy to work, but I had to get used to a totally new environment. And once I found a job, good old Gertrude started charging me rent! Going back to Switzerland started to sound more attractive every day.

Three weeks later, a letter from my father changed things. My dad had met a Swiss guy named Hermann Stocker in Lucerne who owned a restaurant in Houston, Texas, and was looking for a qualified chef. I reached Mr. Stocker by phone. Two days later I was in the air, bound for Texas. I needed to get out of Pennsylvania; I had had it! I stayed a week at Hermann's home in Houston and went to his restaurant every day to observe. My new job would be in San Antonio, where Hermann planned to open a Swiss –type restaurant named the Swiss Chalet. He was entrepreneurial and creative, and he had big plans. He owned another restaurant in Austin and traveled back and forth most of the time. The place in San Antonio was an old country club with a swimming pool, a large bar and club, and three meeting facilities. It looked awful.

It took us some five weeks to give the place a makeover. In the meantime, more help arrived. These included Lucy, an attractive young blonde from Switzerland, who was busy painting the bar; another Swiss who was returning from a failed business venture in Honduras with his Hungarian wife; and a Swiss artist, Ernst Fuchs, and his family, who occupied the apartment in the back of the restaurant. Ernst contributed some of his work to the restaurant. I figured he did that instead of paying rent. He painted some corny-looking mountain scenes, including the Matterhorn, of course. Hired contractors turned the old, rundown country club into a warm-looking chalet.

We put a simple menu together for the time being. It included salads prepared at table with special house vinaigrette, homemade croutons, and cheeses and the usual 1960s appetizers—prawns, onion soup au gratin, and smoked salmon. Our entrees featured Swiss cheese fondue and the very popular fondue Bourguignon with its different sauces and condiments. Different sizes of New York steaks, filet mignons, and steak Diane were finished at the table for additional showmanship. Desserts were delivered by our neighbor Hans Nadler from his Swiss bakery and delicatessen. The warm ambiance, good food, and service of the restaurant made it a popular place where people wanted to meet and be seen. Hermann was very pleased and made money, lots of money.

According to the law at the time, liquor couldn't be served at the table; you had to have a club membership or purchase a guest card for the evening to consume drinks at the bar and nightclub, called the Matterhorn Club. At the time guests were allowed to bring their own bottle to the restaurant and ask for their favorite set-up, such as coke or 7-Up.

Beer and wine was available for dinner. It looked strange to me to see the Dinner guests showing up with their own bottles. Some of our patrons really showed off with liquor bottles in fancy leather casings. It reminded me of movie scenes of the old West.

Lucy made its membership grow like bamboo shoots. She really knew how to at flirt and kept many a clueless fellow hoping all night. Her bar sales were sensational. Nobody knew that she was only 19 years old and was not allowed to serve alcohol. The show band, which included jazz violinist Emilio Caceres, Ted Houston on the piano and the very attractive vocalist Patricia Whitehouse, kept our club busy with a dancing crowd night after night. Little did I knew at the time that Patricia would become the mother of my children, Anthony, Gregory, and Francesca. We met each other for the first time in the kitchen during one of her breaks. She loved guacamole, and a fresh bowl of it with chips became her snack every night she was on duty.

By that time Hermann owned three restaurants, and all three were having a period of great prosperity. It kept us all employed, at least for the time being. He was and still today is an incredible entrepreneur. Maybe he should have been more involved in managing our restaurant. His marriage to Sonya, who ran the Houston business with near-perfect efficiency, began to have its challenges as time went by. Hermann was working to obtain his private pilot's license and purchased an aircraft. He hired a stupendous-looking manager who operated a clothing store downtown but had as much knowledge about our business as a chimney sweep conducting the Metropolitan Opera. Ava, who soon became Hermann's mistress, lived with Lucy in the apartment right behind my kitchen. I did not like her; she was conceited and cocky and thought she was the greatest thing walking this earth. She was conspicuous about her new relationship and many folks began to notice that, which could not be good for business in the long run. It wasn't.

I was not spared from challenges either. I was not a U.S. citizen at the time, and I was ordered by the U.S. Selective Service to report for a physical. At the height of the Vietnam War! I was legally in the country, and obviously that was enough to enlist me in the armed forces. No way, I thought, no more of that! By then, I was in a sound and healthy relationship with Patricia, and come hell or high water, I would never be in the military again. I had done enough of that in Switzerland. Following the advice of a retired air force officer who frequented our restaurant, at my physical I mentioned to the physicians that I had a history of kidney stones. It worked, and I was told that I would to be called for a thorough examination at a later date. I had recently learned that after I turned 26, I won't be called back to enlist again. I was 25 years old and did not want to take the chance of being called back before I turned 26. I didn't want to risk having to go AWOL if the U.S. government called me up.

It was not an easy task to explain to Patricia that I needed to leave the country and return after I turned 26. In early December of 1968, after only eight months in the country, I returned to Switzerland. Patricia and I had an emotional good-bye at the San Antonio airport. We had a meaningful relationship and a lot in common. We felt strongly that our love for one another would endure. My first stop on the way home was Philadelphia, were good old Max was awaiting me at the airport. Even Gertrude showed some excitement as we entered their home in Yardley. We spent a lovely and long weekend together, talking about our very short adventure in Lumberville, this time with genuine smiles on our faces. Four days later, I left by rail for New York City and from there to New York Harbor. I had a one-way ticket to Venice, Italy, aboard the *Leonardo da Vinci*. On board, I encountered a handful of familiar faces, employees of the Swiss Pavilion at the World's Fair of 1968 in San Antonio who were returning home for Christmas. The journey took us to Boston, after which we crossed the Atlantic to Lisbon, Portugal. I loved the feel of that city, where I enjoyed an oversized grilled langoustine, a spiny lobster that the waiters fished out of the live tank at the Gambrinus Restaurant.

Two days later, we entered the harbor of Malaga in Spain, where two of my companions and I had a few too many adult beverages during sightseeing. When we arrived five or six minutes past the boarding time, we were promptly told that we would not be permitted to leave the ship at the next harbor. It was a two-day stop at Naples, and for most Italians on board it was the final destination. Two-thirds of the passengers disembarked there, and many of those who were left went sightseeing to historical places such as Pompeii. The three of us did a lot of sightseeing in the bars of the luxury liner. Messina was next, and then Palermo, where I and some crew members had a memorable shellfish dinner at a small dive in a narrow alley.

After a day in Athens, the journey continued to Venice. From there I traveled by rail to Milan and north to Switzerland, finally arriving in my hometown on Christmas Eve. Chef Rüegsegger spent his winters at the Bürgenstock executive offices in Lucerne. For some years, he had been the full-time corporate chef for the resort, in charge of hiring, purchasing, and administration. He was very happy to see me when I entered his office one afternoon in early January. He wanted to know what had brought me back so quickly. I learned that Tony and Michael had left for Canada. I would never see them again, I thought. There was a wine tasting in progress next door, and the chef invited me to join. Mario was there; he had driven all the way from his home near Lake Como, Italy, to Lucerne for the occasion. Keusch showed up too. He only worked during the summers and had nothing better to do. It really was great to see them again. "I am leaving for Arosa in two weeks," Rüegsegger told me when we returned to his office. "I have to take over the kitchen at the Kulm Hotel in Arosa. The owners asked Mr. Frey if I could step in; their present chef for the season had to be terminated for some unknown reason. Eddie, you are coming with me, I don't know anybody anymore at the hotel, and besides you need a job." Chef Rüegsegger had run the Kulm's kitchens for six or seven winter seasons before assuming his new year-round responsibilities at the Bürgenstock Hotels. I was flattered and so happy not to have to settle for a restaurant job somewhere in the city, pan-frying Wiener schnitzel and grilling bratwurst. Once more, the chef came to my rescue, as he had done two years earlier with the job in Davos. He arranged for my immediate employment at the property.

I was on my way to the resort a couple of days later and started working the day I arrived. It was a great and successful season, and I enjoyed working with Chef Rüegsegger again. A couple of weeks later, the general manager, Mr. Leu, informed us of an upcoming steakhouse promotion sponsored by the U.S. embassy. Rüegsegger and Leu looked at me and said, "Well, we've got the right guy here!" The chef and general manager had hardly any American experience, but then neither did I, since I had spent only a few months in the United States. Nevertheless, they asked me to put a steakhouse menu together for the Stüva

Restaurant. It wasn't that difficult; we found all of our vendors through the embassy, and great-looking prime beef arrived from Chicago soon thereafter. We started to make our own blue cheese dressings and cut our own porterhouse, T-bone, New York, and rib eye steaks and filet mignons. We purchased cases of large Idaho potatoes, and even the iceberg lettuce and cases of Budweiser beer were shipped to us from the United States. It was well advertised too, with three large posters throughout Arosa. It was a huge success. Rüegsegger told me on a visit to Lucerne in the 1970s that they were still doing that steakhouse promo at the Kulm in Arosa.

Hermann came for a visit and did some skiing in Arosa. He loved the steak he ordered at the Stüva. In April I returned with Chef Rüegsegger to the Bürgenstock to open the Taverne Restaurant. Although he offered me a very nice position for the upcoming summer season, I knew I wanted to return to the United States. After all, someone was waiting for me in Texas. In fact, my mind was set on returning to the Lone Star State. While I was staying at the Taverne until the hotels were ready for summer season opening, I was forced to hide one afternoon in an old bathroom at the cellar. I had not registered with the authorities since I had returned to Switzerland. I watched the cop coming up the mountain with his motorcycle and decided it would be better to hide until he was gone again. Hiding behind an old bathtub was not my best moment, but if I had registered with the local authorities, someone most likely would have sent me an order to do another tour of military duty. The cop stopped for a coffee at the restaurant. I couldn't hear what was being said, but I could hear my heart pounding faster. To my relief, I heard him start his motorbike and leave. Coming out from behind that bathtub, I felt like an illegal. Three weeks later, I was in the air, bound for Texas.

Patricia and I were engaged by autumn and planned to wed the following summer. The heyday of the chalet restaurant was over. Lucy's permanent visa failed because her Sugar Daddy, who had bragged many nights over his whiskey about his connections to the right politicians, let her down after he caught her in bed with a hot-shot pilot. Patricia had written me letters that said that the place was not what it used to be, and she was right. On so many occasions, it reminded me of a bad soap opera. Lucy, who was always carefree and full of joie de vivre, eventually left for Switzerland. Ava, who would have been the perfect person to run a brothel instead of a restaurant, somehow disappeared too. The restaurant changed hands, which was not unusual, as I learned while growing up in this business.

Patricia and I were married in Switzerland; the reception was held at Hermann's father's inn outside Lucerne. We spent a month in Europe, enjoying one another and the new chapter in our lives that had begun.

After returning home, we relocated to Houston, where I found employment at the Warwick Hotel, a prestigious and well-managed property. The change in environment was good for both of us. Patricia, who had a degree in nursing from Incarnate Word University in San Antonio, found work at a psychiatric clinic. She was delighted to be working in her profession again. My duties at the Warwick as the chef of the private club on the top floor of the hotel were a far cry from the theatrics of the Swiss Chalet. We enjoyed life, but money was tight. The search for growth was on again, and we realized that we would have to move again in order to find it. Our search brought us seven months later to Minneapolis, Minnesota, literally from the frying pan to the freezer! My wife was skeptical about the move, but after all, you can take a girl out of Texas, but you can't take Texas out of the girl. I found work at the Camelot Restaurant, a busy and well-known eatery in the Twin Cities.

We were really feeling the climate and temperature changes as we finally reached our destination in December in a car that was filled with all of our belongings and our cat. The owner, a short Norwegian named Hans Skalle, welcomed us when we arrived. Hans was very talkative, but at times we could not understand what he was saying because of his heavy Norwegian accent. The

Camelot was a nice old castle surrounded by moats, indeed an impressive-looking eatery for Bloomington, Minnesota. Many celebrities chose to dine at the Camelot, including Carlos Santana, Andy Williams, Vice President Gerald Ford, Hubert Humphrey, and Fritz Mondale.

Patricia and I checked into a room at the newly built Radisson Hotel across the street to freshen up. She was worried about keeping our cat for a couple of nights in a hotel room. The Skalles expected us for dinner by 6:30 that evening. Both of them were astute business people, and their restaurant was in its prime. The bill of fare offered a very good variety of quality food, including prime steaks and fresh seafood such as turbot, salmon, Dover sole and walleye pike, a beloved local favorite. Veal dishes were popular in the seventies. The menu featured seasonal and ethnic specialties, from New England lobster boil to the scrumptious Scandinavian Yule boards. I learned for the first time about the disgusting lutefisk, air-dried cod soaked in a lye solution. The dish was not to my taste, but it was a must at Christmas for the many Scandinavians in Minnesota.

The restaurant offered a very inviting atmosphere. It delivered and promised the impression of dining in an old English castle. Our dinner was great; Patricia had Dover sole, and I had a juicy prime rib. The old fear started to set in; thoughts of my new job began to preoccupy my mind as we listened to all the great ideas and projects of the Skalles. We were introduced to the Camelot's manager, Peter Talbot, a 50-year-old aristocratic-looking Englishman with an enormous rolled-up mustache that extended at least an inch past his cheeks on both sides of his face. His very proper and reserved demeanor impressed both me and Patricia. I got to know him well over the next eighteen months. His hometown of Cheltenham is the same place where we have family. He was a very nice gent.

When Peter observed the operation in the dining rooms, he would continuously roll his mustache while he stood in his favorite spot, where he could see the bar and the large dining area.

I will never forget the busy weekend night when a couple stood up from their lounge seats at the bar, both of them upset and both of them over their limit with alcohol. The overweight husband screamed at Peter: "Do you realize that we have waited over an hour for our table?" Peter, who was never confrontational, did not have an immediate answer. The surly drunk continued his verbal assault: "If we don't have our table in the next five minutes, I'll take you into the alley." Peter's response, while still rolling his whiskers, was "Sir, there is no alley."

An apartment in Edina, less than five minutes from the Camelot, became our new home. This was convenient, since I worked very long hours, anywhere from 11 to 14 hours a day, 300 to 400 covers on weeknights, 900 to 1,000 on Fridays and Saturdays. The place was closed on Sunday. Saturday nights after I made it home, I would fall asleep as soon as I hit the couch. This is almost like Davos, I thought to myself. Since I was a working chef and I also ran the *saucier* station, I was busy most of the night, and expediting all of the orders required great attention. Without fail, Skalle would visit me during the peak of activities. Always dressed in a tailored tuxedo, he would stand next to me with his right arm over a small steamer. He would start a conversation about new ideas and suggestions about what we could do next. He was always very polite, but it became a wearisome obstacle for me. It was not easy to pay full attention to the ongoing service, and now I had to acquire the new talent of paying attention to the boss at the same time! I probably never mastered that task, but I did my best. I never wanted him to feel that I was not paying attention to what he was saying.

When I handed him my resignation after eighteen months, Mr. Skalle was disappointed. I agreed to stay until he found a replacement, which he did after three and a half weeks. I could not turn down the offer to manage the kitchens of the renowned Northstar Inn and its legendary Rosewood Room. The place had an impeccable reputation. IDS Properties owned the place together with the newly built Marquette Inn and the Alumni Club at the top of the IDS Tower. My friend Hans Schaub had offered me his position when he was promoted to director of food and beverages for both hotels.

After eighteen month of working almost alone at the Camelot, I started my new job of managing the kitchens of the five Northstar Restaurants with a staff of 25 chefs. This was a new challenge in my career, and I had to learn much more about how to administer the operation. But many things were well set up by Hans, who was an excellent administrator and a well-organized individual. My counterpart, Werner Zefferer, managed the all the new facilities at the Marquette Inn, located in the IDS Tower. With Hans managing food and beverages at both properties, we developed a sound professional relationship for years to come. The manager of the dining room was very professional, and the fine cuisine brought us numerous awards. I was voted best chef by all my peers in the cities in a survey done by the *Minneapolis Tribune*. Everything was going very well professionally. I had an established crew and plenty of bench strength. The income was good, and since an investment firm owned the properties, we were also rewarded financially if the restaurant met its targets for gross operating profits or food and labor costs.

I loved the challenges of this job and the free hand to make things happen. Our menus were diverse and very popular. We served game specialties in the fall, such as pheasant, venison, wild turkey, and quail. The Rosewood Room remained one of the top restaurants in the Twin Cities. The house specialty of gravlaks, which was carved at the table and served with small boiled potatoes, a fresh dill sauce, and a shot of Aquavit, was the top-selling entrée. This was still the time of the martini lunch, and the general manager and IDS executives never paid attention to the menu before absorbing a couple of martinis when they came for a meal.

Herbert, a 70-year-young German waiter with a slightly arthritic gait, was our dining room comedian. He had an answer for any request a guest might make. When one patron hollered at him "How can I get water in this place?" Herbert's response was "I suggest you put yourself on fire."

Patricia tried her best to get acclimated to "Siberia," as she nicknamed Minnesota. She had a few engagements as a vocalist, sometimes even out of town, and she worked at a bank for a while to help out. But Minneapolis was never her town, and soon she had added "Novosibirsk" to her names for her new home.

We wanted to have children, but nothing was happening. After she visited a psychic, she told me that one day we would have three children. Patricia believed in this; she was very sure about it. But even after six years of marriage, no children. We had tests done and listened to all kind of advice. No success. We finally decided to adopt. To become familiar with adoption procedures, we talked to many parents with adopted kids to learn everything we needed to know. We began to work with a licensed agency and applied to adopt a child from Korea. Home study was needed for all types of adoption, and we began the process. Three or four weeks later, Patricia fell ill. We thought it was the flu. After three days, I accompanied her to the emergency room at Fairview Southdale Hospital, less than two miles from our apartment. She was diagnosed and her problem was quickly indentified. Patricia was pregnant! We knew then that the adoption procedures had had a relaxing effect on her; it had reassured her that she would finally become a mother after waiting for so many years.

We moved to a larger place on France Avenue, across from the library, and began to prepare for an additional family member. Patricia was so happy that she even started to like Siberia and Novosibirsk! On July 13, 1977, Anthony Edward was born. We arranged a nice new baby room for him and planned a trip to Switzerland over Christmas to show off our newest family member. Life was good.

Patricia now a happy and a busy mom, and I was working the usual long hours, six days a week. Good old Max died at the age of 86 in Los Angeles. We started to hear rumors that the hotels might change owners. That is never a good thing when you are settled and content with your job. But there is one certainty in everyone's life, and that is the certainty of change. The rumors became reality in spring of 1978. At least there was plenty of work out there. Mr. Leroy, who was the managing director at our hotels in Minneapolis, returned to Chicago to assume management of the Drake Hotel again. Patricia and I flew to Chicago for several interviews. The first was with Leroy. I liked him, and we had a great dinner at the Cape Cod Room. Although he had an executive chef, he tried to convince me to move there anyway. "I'll give you an office next to Chef, and he'll get the message," Leroy predicted. I remained indecisive for a couple of days because I knew that Patricia would not like Chicago; the city would just be a larger Novosibirsk for her.

We went on to our second interview, this one at a boutique hotel. The Whitehall is an elegant small place, but it was not what I was looking for. We returned to Minneapolis. Skalle started to call, inviting me for lunch. He wanted me to come back. I enjoyed the lunch, but I declined his offer. Many employment opportunities started to open and we had a good choice between several promising places. One was the Kennedy Center for the Performing Arts in Washington, D.C.; another was at a boutique hotel in Carmel, California; a third was at the San Anthony Hotel in San Antonio. Offers also came from the Las Vegas Hilton, the San Francisco Hilton, the Jonathan Club in Los Angeles—I don't remember all of them.

Patricia and I flew to Chicago again for an initial interview for the Kennedy Center job, and it went very well. I was cleared to visit the center in Washington, D.C. We liked the city. The interview with the director of operations the following day went well too. As with the job in Chicago, the executive chef was still there, and as I toured the kitchen I quickly decided that it was not the place for me. Patricia and I ate perfectly cooked and very tasty paella at a Spanish restaurant in the nation's capital that night.

As I traveled by myself to San Antonio a week later, I knew in advance that the San Anthony would not be a go. But I went for

Patricia and for her parents, who lived in San Antonio. They would have loved to have seen their daughter back home. The interview was a total waste of time. The owners of the hotel had hired a management consulting firm. They wanted to get rid of the chef (among other management staff), but the general manager wanted to keep him. There was even conflict about who should interview me. Some human resources guy insisted that he should do the interview, but the general manager said, "No, it's going to be me, I am still in charge." The hired consultants who were running all over the property felt that they needed to talk to me too. It was a mess. I spent a day with my in-laws, who were understandably disappointed, and then I returned to Minneapolis.

5. A Growing Family, a Flourishing Career

After the interview in San Antonio, I flew to California for an interview at the Pine Inn in Monterey. When I arrived at the airport in San Francisco, my friend Herbert was waiting for me. We had worked in Houston together, but I had met him for the first time when he was employed as a baker for Nadler's Bakery on San Pedro Avenue in San Antonio, near the chalet restaurant. Herbert always put some extra kirsch in my tortes when the owner, Hans Nadler, wasn't looking. Hans was very stingy and made my friend pay for any little bit of food he ate at the bakery. When Herbert delivered the desserts to my kitchen, I would prepare a good dinner for him; he looked too skinny to me.

Now Herbert was managing the pastry operation for United Airlines. We drove to his apartment in San Mateo, where I spent the night. I flew to Monterey the following day. The interview went well, but the Pine Inn was a small place that was kind of old, and one of the family members was the chef. He probably wanted to get out of the kitchen, and I couldn't blame him when I saw the facility.

I was getting calls about jobs at home, and Patricia was leaving messages with Herbert while I was in California. It was somehow a little complicated before cell phones. Herbert called me at the Pine Inn to tell me that Patricia had received a call from the San Francisco Hilton for an immediate interview. When I called Patricia to hear more, she told me that both the San Francisco Hilton and Hilton's corporate office in Beverly Hills had called. Herbert picked me up again at the airport in San Francisco as I returned from Monterey.

When I arrived for my interview at the San Francisco Hilton, Werner Lewin was sitting in a leather chair in his office speaking German on the telephone. I stood there for a while until he gestured for me to sit down. I listened to an interesting conversation, Werner of course not knowing that I spoke the language. As I looked at the walls in his office, I saw countless pictures of him and his younger brother Henri with celebrities, including Sinatra, Jerry Lewis, Liberace, past presidents, the Hilton family, and German chancellors. Everyone who was anyone was on that wall. Werner finally got off the phone, shook my hand, and began the interview.

Werner Lewin and his brother Henri had escaped Nazi Germany and had made it to Shanghai, where they made their living working in nightclubs and restaurants. In 1947, the brothers had come to the United States and moved to San Francisco, where they found employment at the Fairmont Hotel. They moved their way up the ranks, and soon they were managing the Fairmont and had an office next to the office of Ben Swig, the owner.

The brothers got in touch with an old school friend, Peter Goldman, who was working in New York. Werner and Henri persuaded him to join them in San Francisco. In 1964, after the brothers had bitter disagreements with Ben Swig, they moved a few blocks downhill to O'Farrell Street to manage the newly built San Francisco Hilton. Peter Goldman became the Fairmont's managing director. The brothers were protégés of Konrad Hilton and worked their way into the highest executive positions. In 1972, Henri had been appointed executive vice president of the Hilton's gaming interests in Las Vegas, and he spent most of his time there. Werner was the vice president and general manager of the San Francisco Hilton Hotel.,

I had had conversations with people in the industry who had advised me not to work for the Lewins. One well-known San Francisco chef had warned me with the words "All they do is work the living shit out of you and when they're tired of you, they give you the boot." Henri had been accused of making shady deals and playing favorites with union officials in Las Vegas and was the subject of an ongoing grand jury investigation. No one I had talked to had had anything nice to say about them. I knew that the chef at the San Francisco Hilton was gone because he was recuperating from a heart attack.

Despite all the negativity and warnings, I still wanted this job. I wanted a huge property on my résumé, and I got it. The pay was very good, and I liked San Francisco. My starting date would be May 11, 1978.

After a night out for dinner with Herbert at Trader Vic's, I flew back to Minneapolis. I was only 34 years old. On May 6, I began the drive from Minneapolis to the West Coast to start my new job, leaving Patricia and ten-month-old Tony behind temporarily. I reached San Francisco on May 9. After I had settled into my living quarters, I showered and freshened up; I was tired from the three-day road trip. Then I called Hans Lauer, a corporate chef with Hilton who had been filling the gap at the Hotel until I reached San Francisco. Hans and I met in the coffee shop. It was great to see him again; we knew each other from a few years back, when I had visited Dallas, where Hans had been the executive chef at the Statler Hilton. Hans, a pleasant and hardworking German, had also worked years ago in Engelberg, where he met his wife. He has opened many of Hilton's hotels, and now he was a traveling chef, going from city to city and convention to convention.

Hans gave me an extensive tour of the kitchens and introduced me to all the chefs and cooks on duty. I realized that with a culinary staff of 97, it would take me days to get to know them all. Hans and I had dinner at the Chef's Table Restaurant, an old and very outdated place in the hotel's lobby level. The restaurant was virtually empty. I thought the menu was disgusting, as did Hans. "That's what the Lewins want," he said. "They want to have a menu that features items they like personally." Great marketing! I thought. Hans filled me in on other important details, such as the strength of the local union and what I could and could not expect while working for Werner and Henri. Werner joined us for a few minutes at our table, dressed in an immaculately tailored suit, and told me that his brother Henri would be in San Francisco by the next day. I had heard so many stories about Henri that I could hardly wait for the encounter. Maybe he was not as bad as colleagues had told me, or maybe he truly was impossible to work for. I had heard that he was flamboyant; he would call you in the middle of the night for something trivial. I knew that Henri walked that thin line between genius and crazy.

 I didn't sleep well at all that night; I had my usual healthy dose of anxiety before starting a new job. Hans would be at my side for another week, and that reduced my anxiety somewhat. The next morning, I began to get to know some of the staff. Inga was my administrative assistant, charming, punctual and very efficient. She did the weekly schedules for the culinary and stewarding crews and the entire kitchen payroll with a pencil; there were no computer programs. My office was hidden behind the restaurant, a few steps up from the main floor of the kitchen. There was one desk for Inga and one for me and a television set mounted on the wall. A small round table was always neatly set up for our meals and coffee breaks. The kitchen was departmentalized into a production area, the *garde manger*, the pantry, the pastry shop, a restaurant line, and the butcher shop. At the far end was a relative tiny coffee shop kitchen and the room service office. The employee cafeteria was located one floor down. On the top floor of the Hilton Tower was the legendary Henri's Room, a large restaurant with a magnificent view of San Francisco. Max, our *sous chef,* was a production machine, and it was hard for me to imagine how the place could operate without him. His reliability and time management were second to none. Every large convention hotel needs a Max to expedite such a large volume of production.

As Inga was briefing me on the payroll procedures and all the different union classifications and wages, the phone on my desk rang. It was Henri. "Get up here young man, I want to get acquainted with you!" he said, and hung up. Henri's office on the second floor was at least three or four times larger than Werner's office behind the front desk. All four walls were covered with the kind of pictures I had seen in his brother's office. Henri's office featured three large aquariums, and I counted five telephones on his huge mahogany desk. The place reminded me of an antiques store. Henri was entertaining, a first-class raconteur, very funny. Most of our half-hour conversation was about him, and why not? He was number three in the Hilton hierarchy and as the senior vice president of the gaming division; he generated massive profits for the hotel chain. As I left his office, somewhat bedazzled, I knew that I would be called into his sanctuary often.

Hans left a week later, and I was on my own. I had taken many notes during the time Hans was with me. He had given me numerous suggestions about how to deal with the brothers. "They have weird tastes," Hans said. "Two items you need to have available at any time are chicken soup and lentil soup; these are essential. Whenever Henri or Werner make their rounds, they will taste your soup of the day. If they don't like it, they'll ask you to make chicken soup or lentil soup."

I really loved the job and its professional challenges. My relationships with the rank-and-file staff members were good. I respected them and most of them respected me. When I slipped, I was challenged immediately, believe me.

Dealing with the Lewins was a whole different story. This was something I had to learn to endure. The short length of service of the numerous former executive chefs was evidence of how challenging this part of the job was. Preparing a special dinner for the family became a much more difficult task than preparing a banquet for 2,000 people.

There was no food and beverage director at our large property. Frank Karliner, the director of catering, also filled this role. When corporate insisted that such a large property had to have a food and beverage director, the brothers would hire one, only to run him or her out of there within six months. This is what they did with Carlo Bicacci, a very nice Italian with plenty of experience. Carlo was an absolute wreck after six months on the job as their whipping boy. All of the executives at the San Francisco Hilton were totally controlled by Werner and Henri. Frank Karliner, who had lived with them in Shanghai, apparently was grateful to them and did whatever he had to do, even the impossible. He and I became good friends, and he often had dinner in my office before he walked to the train station on his way home to San Jose.

After I had lived for five weeks in a hotel room, I had to get out of there and find a place for my family to live. The Lewins didn't like that; they wanted to have access to me around the clock. I wasn't able to afford the pricey real estate in the Bay Area, but I found a lovely house to rent in Walnut Creek. One month later, Patricia and Anthony arrived. I was very happy, but the Lewins weren't; they argued that I was too far away from the job. It was a relief to move out of the hotel when my family arrived.

Henri usually left Las Vegas on Thursdays to come home to San Francisco, returning to Las Vegas again on Monday morning. Slowly I learned Henri's method of testing me, usually on Saturday mornings as he arrived in his office. First he would make sure I was at work by calling me at the office. Then he would summon me to his office, where I would get some kind of culinary lesson and listen to complaints he had allegedly received from guests. Then we would plan a dinner menu for his family for that night. Usually these dinners were for Werner and Henri and their wives and the Goldmans. (By this time, Peter Goldman was working for Hyatt.) Some of Henri's favorite foods were grilled New York strip sirloin with beef marrow, roasted shallots, and a red wine demiglace sauce. Grilled salmon with egg sauce was another favorite. When I made this for him for the first time, I served it with a Hollandaise sauce, which, so far as I knew, was an egg sauce! Henri walked into the kitchen with his plate and said, "Chef, this fucking sauce you served me would not even be suitable for greasing airplane wheels." That was my first unpleasant encounter with Henri. "Is this going to happen every week?" I wondered.

On the weekends, they ate at Peter Goldman's place at the Embarcadero Hyatt. This always felt like a night off to me, but sometimes I would get a phone call from Chef Chris at the Embarcadero: "What's this guy's problem? I am glad I don't work at your place!" Henri actually made me laugh the night he stormed into the kitchen, again with his plate in his hand, and told me in front of everyone: "Chef, have a look at this; the Nazis tried to poison me with food every day when I was in the concentration camp in Auschwitz, but they never succeeded! You think you will?" I knew that Henri was never at Auschwitz. He loved to play the comedian. One of my night-shift *sous chefs* was so afraid of Henri that he would lock himself in a walk-in refrigerator as soon as he heard his voice.

One night Frank Karliner told me about the twelve-course Chinese dinner he had sold to a group of 250 people. I wasn't an expert on Chinese food, and the thought of this event gave me a headache. But I had several excellent Chinese chefs on staff, and they know how to make this party a success. Karliner and I went to a Chinese restaurant where he had ordered the exact menu we were planning to prepare, so we could see and taste the food. All of the courses had to be French served. On the night of the event, we were in very good shape; everything was under control. The Chinese chefs on staff did a remarkable job. Our sixth or seventh course was egg foo young with shrimp. All of the servings were neatly arranged on sheet pans, ready to go into the rotating oven. Everything was going very smoothly until we fired the egg foo youngs. Something happened in our rotating oven, and all sheet pans flipped over. All of the fried egg patties were history! I ran down to the main kitchen and grabbed Lee, our line chef, and two others. With no time to explain what had just happened, I gave the guys 15 minutes to have 250 of the mini-omelets ready. The velocity and determination of the three Chinese chefs was a miracle. The course was served with only a few minutes' delay. Frank Karliner and I drank a bottle of wine after dinner that night and felt fortunate that the accident hadn't occurred while we were serving the Peking duck.

I received a salary increase after a year with the Hilton, and it came at just the right time. Patricia was pregnant again and happy as she could be. On May 14, 1979, our second son, Gregory James, was born at John Muir Medical Center in Walnut Creek. I treasured the very little time I was able to spend at home with my little family of four. My dad finally made it to California for a visit at the age of 84. I managed to take a few days off for travel and sightseeing, and we had a great time. I am so glad that I decided to accompany Dad on his flight home to Switzerland so I could spend a few more days with him. That was the last time I saw him.

In 1980, contract negotiations with the hotel workers' union failed, and in July, Local 2 began a citywide strike. For the first time in forty years, a major labor dispute began to wreak havoc in San Francisco's hotel industry; workers at thirty-six hotels had walked out. We didn't know how long it was going to last. The Lewins ordered us to shut down the hotel. We gave the perishable food to local soup kitchens, the Salvation Army, and St. Anthony's Dining Room. Two days later, Barron Hilton, Konrad Hilton's son, called and ordered us to reopen immediately. We had to purchase just about everything we had given away. One thousand rooms were reopened, but the Tower remained closed. Help arrived quickly from the corporate office, including Peter Kleiser, our regional food and beverage executive for the entire West Coast; Joe Shaefer, director of food technology; Hans Lauer; a couple of *sous chefs* from the Beverly Hilton; and Mike, a banquet chef from the Waldorf Astoria in New York. Mike was the perfect workhorse; we needed him to replace Max, who was carrying signs in front of our hotel. We also hired a few scabs for positions we had to fill. We were all locked in; nobody could go home. For how long, nobody had a clue.

Because Patricia was pregnant with our third child and was caring for our two small children alone, I sent her home to San Antonio. It was a good decision; the strike lasted almost five weeks. We served breakfast, lunch, and dinner buffets every day for 600 to 1,000 guests. "Maybe this is going to be another Davos," I feared. Henri stormed into the kitchen a few days into the walkout to yell and complain about the mayor: "Did you guys hear what Feinstein said? [He actually said Fine Swine.] She suggested that we give them what they want so the strike could end. That shows you what a stupid bitch she is."

The picketers were very active all night long. Produce and other provisions had to be picked up in a van with a police escort at designated areas in the city. No one delivered; no one would cross the picket lines, except for Andy Knox from the Parisian Bakery. Frank Karliner booked a banquet at the last minute one Saturday afternoon during the strike, and I found myself with no sourdough bread in the house. I called Andy and asked him how he was planning to get the bread into the hotel. He said "Not to worry, I have my ways." Two hours later, I saw him walking through the kitchen with a scab bellman and four suitcases loaded on the bell cart. Clever Andy had checked himself as a guest into the hotel with suitcases full of fresh bread!

It was a stressful time; the hours were very long while we were locked in. We usually took turns cooking dinner for ourselves, and we set up a nice chef's table every night, when things started to slow down around nine. One night Hans would cook, and another night it would be Peter Kleisers, Joe Schaefer, Waldorf Astoria Mike, or me.

As the labor dispute continued and turned more violent, SWAT team members from the San Francisco Police Department were positioned at some of the vulnerable spots throughout the hotel, which was the size of a city block. Two of them were assigned to the kitchen. At our bi-weekly meetings in Henri's sanctuary, he would keep us up to date about negotiations. He would turn on his TV so we could see the activities outside. Everybody wanted to go home; the strike had made all of us very weary. Henri shut me right up when I had a small disagreement with him at one of his meetings; "Chef, what's the color of the chair you sitting on?" he hollered from behind his desk. "Brown," I answered. "No, it is white! When Henri says it's white, it is white! Got that?" I backed down, realizing that no one argues with Henri; you would lose every time.

The labor dispute lasted some four and a half weeks, and when it was over both sides claimed victory. With Max on duty again, our kitchen was fully operational the day after the strike ended. I finally made it home to Walnut Creek to check on the house and get it ready for my wife and children to return. As I was working, the phone rang. I knew it was the hotel. I just felt it. Werner was at the other end of the line and wanted to know where I was. "Business doesn't stop after the strike," he said. "I expect you back at the hotel tonight, chef."

One Thursday afternoon, Henri returned from Las Vegas and entered the kitchen, asking the usual question: "Chef, do you have any fresh fish?" "I do, Henri; we have some very fresh steelhead salmon." That was one of his favorites. We grilled a couple of pieces, and Lee, my line chef, prepared that perfect egg sauce with it. Henri was sitting in a booth in the back of the restaurant with his girlfriend. I wanted to make sure that he was happy with his meal and paid a visit to his table. At that moment, I saw Henri's wife entering the restaurant. So did Henri. Grabbing his plate and attaché case, he quickly sat down in the opposite booth and continued to eat his salmon. Before Mrs. Lewin made it to the back, Henri ordered me to sit very close to his female companion and hold her hand. "Act as if you're in love, god damn it!" I did it, but I felt very awkward. Mrs. Lewin sat down at her husband's table, telling him that she had been looking for him all over. "I just stopped at the hotel to get a bite to eat," Henri lied, "and you can see with your own eyes what I found! Our chef, sitting with his girlfriend in my restaurant, holding hands and feeding her on the house!" The Lewins left and his mistress did too a few minutes later, leaving me sitting in the booth, amazed at what had just happened!

When Werner went on a ten-day vacation in Florida, Henri stayed at the San Francisco property. One day I saw him having a lengthy conversation on the phone near the kitchen at his restaurant at the top of the Tower. I knew he was going to have dinner, so I decided to wait to talk to him. To my surprise, when he got off the phone, he asked me to join him for dinner. Henri ordered lentil soup, an item I had to have ready every day, followed by "Henri's roasted chicken," one of his famous dishes. To make it simple, I ordered the same. As we were eating, he told me that he had had a lengthy conversation with his brother in Florida. They had discussed making cutbacks because business still was soft after the labor dispute. The restaurant had two show bands; one of them played from 7 p.m. to 10 p.m., the second from 9 to midnight. From 9 to 10, both bands performed together. Henri told me that Werner was losing sleep in Florida because he couldn't decide which band to lay off. "My brother is a total idiot," Henri said. "I had to make the decision for him, me again, Genius Henri! I told him to fire both bands and hire a new one!"

In early December of 1980 Patricia checked into the John Muir Medical Center to give birth to our daughter Francesca. I rushed to Werner's office to announce the happy event. He smiled and told me that he had five kids. When my wife was ready to give birth, I called a taxi to take her to the hospital. But when I was getting ready to leave for the hospital, Werner told me "We have work to do and you need to be at the hotel, not at the hospital. We are very busy today, chef, you need to stay here!" I could not believe his words, and they triggered an angry reaction in me. I used some language I probably should have avoided, but it felt good. I left the office and drove across the Bay to witness the birth of Francesca on December 4, 1980.

My relationship with the Lewins worsened after my encounter with Werner. They knew very well how to push my buttons and were very good at doing it. When I fell ill one Saturday night with a fever and a sore throat, I visited Werner's office again to tell him I need to go home. Once again he argued that the hotel was too busy for me to leave. "Besides, we have dinner with the Goldmans later on tonight." I left for home and went straight to bed. A minor earthquake woke me up around 9 p.m., when I heard some objects falling from a shelf. I got up, but there was no damage; it was just a small tremor. I went back to bed and the phone rang. It was Henri, of course: "Chef, where are you, we had an earthquake!" "No kidding," I thought to myself. "My elevators are out of commission at the hotel, you are sick, and our dinner took too long. How can I continue to operate this hotel when I am surrounded by a bunch of numbskulls? I tried your soup of the day and it was cold!" "Well, heat it up," I replied, and hung up the phone. At that moment I had had it with all of the insults and harassment.

I decided to look for something else. Life is too short, and it was time for a change. Three days later, Joe Shaefer asked me to join Hans Lauer to work the Super Bowl at the New Orleans Hilton. For ten days I had relief from the Lewins. I began to schedule interviews at the headquarters of Stouffer's in Cleveland, Ohio. The day I landed in Cleveland was cold, windy, and snowy; it reminded me of Minneapolis. The offered me the opening job at their new property in Itasca, near Chicago, and I accepted. But when I returned to sunny California, I declined the offer. It was not a good idea to move my family back to the Midwest. I decided to stay in San Francisco, and I accepted a job at the Sir Francis Drake Hotel. The hotel was small and old, but it would do it for now. I didn't particularly like the job, but at least the hours were much better and I was never called at home to ask me why I was not at work.

Three months later, Hans Pluntke, the corporate food and beverages executive for the Princess Hotel, asked me to travel with him to Acapulco. I spent eight days at the magnificent resort properties of that hotel, observing everything I could, and I was very impressed. After a long interview, Managing Director Vincent Carrozza offered me the position of executive chef there. Carrozza told me that he had heard only good things about me and that Joe Shaefer had recommended me highly. I was flattered. I returned to San Francisco and discussed the offer with Patricia. We decided that Acapulco was not the place to go with three little kids. I'm grateful today that we made that decision. Ten years later, Carrozza was abducted by some by gunmen dressed in federal police uniforms.

Hans Pluntke assured me that there would be something else for me in the near future. "Maybe Bermuda," he said. "In the meantime, we'll keep you on the back burner."

One day when I was sitting in my small, dark, and dusty office at the Drake, doing some paperwork, I answered the phone and heard the voice of Kurt Stielhack, Hyatt's corporate chef, at the other end of the line. "What are you doing in that shitty old dump? You must be nuts! Come on over, I want to talk something over with you." "Where are you, Kurt?" I asked. "Next door at Union Square Hyatt. Get your ass over here! We'll pop open a bottle of champagne." Kurt, a good-looking guy with a sparkling personality, was dressed in his usual blue jeans and red shirt. He was happy to finally meet me, and I was happy to see him for the first time. We knew each other from previous phone conversations, but we had never met in person. He had been after me for some time to join the Hyatt. He showed me pictures of Hyatt's innovative food programs as we sat in his hotel suite sipping champagne. Before he joined the Hyatt, Kurt had been the executive chef for a year and a half at the San Francisco Hilton. "Eddie," he said, "you must be glad to be out of hell!" "Don't even start me on that one," I replied. Kurt continued: "Now let's talk about a new hotel under construction in San Antonio. We had one of our own chefs in mind for that place, but he left the company. Now we are looking on the outside. We are looking at you, Eddie. I've asked you on a few occasions to work for us, and now I expect you to take our offer." It sounded good, and I thought of how delighted Patricia would be to return to her hometown. I didn't tell Kurt that my wife was from San Antonio, but he found out a few days later and sent Patricia a huge flower arrangement, welcoming her back to San Antonio! That strategy worked. "I follow up with you," Kurt said. "I want you to take a weekend off from the dump where you're working, fly to San Antonio, and meet the opening general manager."

Sigi Brauer, the opening food and beverage director, was waiting for me when I arrived at the airport in San Antonio. We drove straight downtown to the hotel's pre-opening office at the old Landmark building, where Norm Howard, the general manager assigned to San Antonio's new Hyatt Regency Hotel, welcomed me home. A room was reserved for me at the St. Anthony Hotel, where I had experienced that alienating and confusing interview a few years earlier. Norm, Sigi, and I had a great dinner of roasted duck in a fig sauce at the Four Seasons that night. As I went to bed that night, I was excited about the prospect of opening a new hotel, and I had been assured that it would be a very busy place.

The sticking point was the salary; salaries in San Francisco are much higher than they are San Antonio! Going backward in terms of income was not an option. And I didn't believe all that "lower cost of living" rhetoric. Eventually the issue was resolved and I got what I asked for, but not before Norm referred to me as a "Swiss Jew." My starting date was set for October 1, 1981. After ten long and interesting years, we finally closed the loop and returned to Texas. I met my first "Hyatt people" as we started our jobs and prepared for the opening of the city's newest hotel. Norman was a forward-thinking man with an intellectual approach. We loved working for him. What a difference from what I had had to endure in San Francisco. The opening was a great success. Patricia and I purchased our first home.

In March of 1984, I received an early morning phone call from my sister in Switzerland to tell me that Dad had passed on. I was able to get to Switzerland in time to gather with the family to say good-bye, and I promised myself to return more often to visit my mother.

Changes in our lives never end; one year later, Hyatt's corporate office called me and asked me to move to Dallas. As I started my new assignment, I was quite worried about Patricia's health. She knew that something was not right, despite the doctor's reassurance that everything seemed to be fine. We put our home in San Antonio on the market. Soon another health issue visited our family. Our son Gregory was diagnosed with juvenile diabetes at the age of six. Because of her training as a nurse, Patricia recognized the symptoms and had him hospitalized at once. Soon he was stabilized, and Patricia knew how to measure blood sugar levels and administer insulin shots.

In early January of 1986, I was on my way to Puerto Rico as part of a team to help "Hyattize" the newly acquired Cerromar and Dorado Beach Hotels. When I returned from the Caribbean, a new hotel manager joined the Dallas Hyatt with the last name of Lewin. Jerry was Henri's oldest son. I knew him well; we had played indoor soccer together. Jerry told me that his father and his uncle had both left the Hilton. At first, the managing director of the Hyatt, Tim Lindgren, and young Lewin had some difficulties. One night when Jerry and I went to see a Mavericks game at the Reunion Arena, he expressed his frustration: "Eddie, you know my Dad very well. We all know he is crazy, but I think Lindgren definitely is crazier than my Dad." I saw Henri again when he came to visit his son in Dallas. Naturally he had a funny comment ready for me the moment I met him in the atrium of the hotel: "I just saw an ambulance leaving the hotel with two dozen guests suffering from food poisoning and immediately knew that you must be the chef here!" Henri hadn't changed a bit! He was always a comedian.

One year later, just as we started to enjoy the new home we had purchased in Dallas, Patricia was diagnosed with cancer. Two months later, both her breasts had to be removed in a double radical mastectomy at Baylor University Medical Center. She needed lots of support and moved back to San Antonio to live with her parents. There was really no alternative. She started her chemotherapy treatments while still taking care of three small children. Life changed drastically in our family.

At first I commuted between Dallas and San Antonio, but after three months, I was very grateful to get my job back in San Antonio. The children were taken care of, Gregory was stable, and even Patricia began to show some signs of improvement. We all lived in the hotel while we waited to move into our newly purchased home near Bulverde. The house was in a quiet neighborhood, and we loved it. The whole family prayed for Patricia's recovery. But when I returned home from work one evening in early October, Patricia was having difficulty breathing, and I called 911. She was hospitalized immediately. The family gathered around her hospital bed, Francesca, Tony, and Greg crawling on top of it, holding their mom's hand. She smiled despite all the pain she was in. With a firm grip and for the last time, Patricia held on to her three children.

The Peyer Family

The hotel was extremely busy that weekend, and I had to be at work early that Sunday morning, October 25th, 1987. The call I feared so much came at noon: Patricia had left us for good. I was immediately confronted with an overwhelming number of new issues, and at first it was very difficult to go on. Ladies from the church watched the kids after school until I could get home from work. I found a full-time housekeeper; Elrose was there every day to cook dinner for the children. That brought me some relief, and life went on—it had to. Managing Greg's diabetes was a new challenge for me. My learning curve was very steep; I mistakenly gave him an overdose of insulin and had to call 911 once more. We spent Christmas that year in Los Angeles with Norm Howard and his family. Ron Agron, our new general manager, came unannounced to my home several times just to vacuum my house. Sue Sucin, our human resources director, took the kids to see movies, decorated the Christmas tree, and was always ready to babysit. My witty and very funny companion Patrick Donelly, a

South African who was our food and beverage director, always made us laugh with his unusual sense of humor. Normalcy had somehow returned by the time I participated in the opening of Hyatt's new Waikoloa properties in Hawaii. Greg had learned to inject himself with insulin, and I called daily from the islands to determine what dosage he needed. Life continued.

In May 1991, I went to New Zealand to help the Hyatt people in Auckland with an authentic Mexican fiesta promotion. It was sponsored by American Airlines, the City Council of Auckland, and, believe it or not, Weight Watchers International. I had just married again, and the trip was also my honeymoon with Carmen. It took us two hours to get all the equipment we had brought through customs, but we finally made it to the Hyatt Regency Auckland, located across from the University of Auckland. Tom Pasha, the director of sales at the San Antonio Hyatt; Tom's wife; and Santiago, one of my Mexican chefs, were also with us. The ballroom of the hotel had been decorated as almost an exact replica of the Alamo Plaza in San Antonio. They had done an incredible job. The three-week-long promotion started after we mastered a few challenges, such as finding some of the necessary foods and spices. The outstanding culinary staff at the Hyatt Regency helped make the promotion a huge success. The few American professors at the University of Auckland were ecstatic to find Mexican food. They missed that familiar taste from home and often had to satisfy their craving with spicy Asian fare, which was readily available in New Zealand. We were stunned when actress Cybill Shepherd showed up to enjoy lunch. "I just had a craving for Mexican food," she told us.

Two days after we returned to San Antonio, I was on my way to Europe again, together with a handful of other Hyatt chefs, all winners of a bistro promotion. That particular journey meant ten days of drinking wine and eating French foods, from Paris to Reims and the Burgundy region. "This would be a perfect way to develop gout," I thought. As we all partied in the city of Beaune, I had had enough of foie gras and fine wines. We were close to

Switzerland, and I felt the need to see my mother. I took a train from Dijon to Lausanne, where my sister Vreni was waiting to drive me to Lucerne. My visit was very short and sweet because I had to join my wine buddies a few days later at Charles de Gaulle in Paris to fly back to the States. Two short years later, I made it just in time to Lucerne on Christmas Eve. Mom died a few hours later on Christmas Day morning at the age of 93.

I had experienced a taste of America's premier sports event during Super Bowl XV in 1981 at the New Orleans Hilton. I remember the various VIP functions we had to host and the intensity of getting the pre-game brunch ready for 3,000 people on that January Sunday. I recall the exquisite small barbecue Hans Lauer and I delivered to Barron Hilton's private jet for his return flight to Los Angeles. In 1993, while I was working in San Antonio, I received marching orders for Super Bowl XXVII at the Rose Bowl in Pasadena, California. I arrived at Burbank Airport on January 26, 1993. A small army of Hyatt chefs, food and beverage executives, and catering people checked into a hotel in Burbank. We were all getting ready for a massive event, the NFL commissioner's reception for 6,000 people on the Friday night before the game. That was Act I. We also had to prepare for the various large receptions in the tents of corporate sponsors before and after game time in front of the Rose Bowl on Sunday. The commissioner's party was at the Burbank Equestrian Center in air-conditioned tents; the party was the size of two city blocks. A small kitchen at a culinary school one football field away from the tent city served as the preparation site for the commissioner's party. This was not exactly an easy task, as massive amounts of food arrived every day at this site in the days leading up to Friday's party. The executive chef from our Budapest Hyatt had the lovely assignment of roasting 8,000 pieces of chicken in a small single convection oven with only five shelves. The Hungarian and his Serbian *sous-chef* worked alternately for some 34 hours to complete the job. Both of them resembled and behaved like chickens as they finished their monotonous mission. After a day's rest, both of them returned to Budapest. I worked the barbecue and southwestern food buffet together with two guest chefs. We struggled to meet our deadline for Friday afternoon. We prepped and sliced some 100 smoked beef briskets; 1,000 pounds of barbecued pork ribs; some 3,000 smoked sausages; countless burritos, tacos, and quesadillas; and 400 pounds of, bless the Lord, already mashed avocados for guacamole. Schlepping all the prepared food from our kitchen at the culinary school to the tent location made for an unattractive sight. A local sausage maker from Los Angeles who was very eager to help provided us with an oversized mobile convection oven to reheat some of the food before it was placed on various buffets. That piece of equipment looked more like a lunar module simulator than an oven, but it helped.

Other buffet stations featured Italian fare with great antipasti and cheese displays, risotto, pasta, and veal scallopini, all of it action-cooked to order. The dessert tables were scrumptious, offering a variety of flavors of crème brulée, its sugar torched in front of the guests. Delectable sushi and iced shellfish displays and an extravagant deli and charcuterie setup completed the bill of fare for some 5,000 attendees. Then NFL commissioner Paul Tagliabue and our illustrious Hyatt corporate chef, Janos Kiss, did a walkthrough and inspection half an hour before the doors opened. It was indeed an impressive show. A beautiful and elevated section served a family-style dinner for all the NFL owners and their invited guests.TV personalities, radio talk show hosts, numerous Hollywood stars, many former NFL players, and of course politicians were easily recognized at each of the 120 tables. Prime beef tenderloin, Alaskan salmon, and roasted chicken were skillfully presented by over sixty waiters and waitresses. There were massive amounts of food left as the event ended that found its way to numerous food banks.

We enjoyed a short break and a cold beer then jumped into vans that took us to the Rose Bowl for a meeting and corporate tent assignments for Sunday's game between the Dallas Cowboys and the Buffalo Bills. It was chilly that night in southern California. The Toyota corporate tent was my assignment, and I was not too happy when I learned that Toyota had scheduled two events--a pre-game party and a postgame party! 600 people each. Many of us still were sorting through refrigerators, searching for all the foods we needed, and studying the menus as temperatures fell into the mid-thirties. On game day, we arrived in our vans at the Rose Bowl by seven in the morning. An old building adjacent to the corporate village served as the storage area for all kitchen utensils. Some thirty chefs started running toward that building as someone opened its doors. They looked like a bunch of savage barbarians storming a building. The first one there picked the best utensils and pots and pans. I was slow that morning and had to make do with the few utensils left.

I was happy to meet the lady who ran the front of the house for the two events, Terry Rack, a very experienced food and beverage manager. She had worked for a couple of years at our hotel in San Antonio. I knew that Terry was sharp and would do a great job. Both of us were glad to be partners for the events. A young female apprentice chef and a cook from the Long Beach Hyatt were the only help assigned to me. I began to feel stress, just like that first day on the job at the Suvretta House in St. Moritz. It took us some time to get familiar with our field kitchen. Some 3,000 pieces of very appetizing sushi and mountains of Alaskan king crab legs, their shells already cracked, were delivered at noon time. We began to build our submarine sandwiches on slices of fresh sourdough bread, tossed all the salads, and fired cured hams on the bone and meatloaf for the post-game party. The pre-game event went over without any hiccups. During game time I grilled 40 whole beef tenderloins on an eight-foot charcoal grill outside our tent while my assistants filled bowls with condiments, trimmed the hams, and sliced meatloaf. Terry used a spectacular Harley Davidson theme to decorate the dining room. Michael Jackson was a few feet away from our site in his dressing-room tent, getting ready for a spectacular half-time performance.

We were ready as the game ended. Some people started to show up earlier while the Cowboys were still humiliating the Bills. I asked our young apprentice chef to carve the roasted tenderloin at the buffet. Everything seemed just perfect. I went to inspect the buffet after about 15 minutes and noticed with horror that each guest's plate loaded with thick and juicy tenderloin slices that were at least 7 ounces each. "Holy shit," I thought, "in ten minutes there won't be any tenderloin left!" I immediately took over the carving. I was mad at myself because I had failed to tell the girl how to portion the beef. Once she started the big cuts, everyone else expected the same portion. My first slice was for an unhappy-looking, big-bellied guy (most likely a Bills fan) who was already licking his chops. He got a quarter-inch slice. I will never forget the perplexed look on his face as he said, "What the fuck is this, you asshole?" I had no choice and quickly paid attention to the line of people behind him. "Next, please," I said. We made it with the beef, but barely.

Fourteen years after I joined the Hyatt, Tony, my oldest son, was seventeen. My hair was turning gray, proof that I reached 50 years of age. My work was my priority; at times I felt it was too much of a priority. Life started to fly by. Lucy, the vivacious young woman from the Swiss Chalet restaurant, came for visits with her family at least every other year. She had married and had two beautiful children. Hermann Stocker moved back to Switzerland and bought a historic inn near Lucerne. Today, he frequently visits San Antonio, since all of his children still live in Texas. A phone call from the past awakened old memories; it was Michael Durrer. He had found me on the internet, but it was Tony, my roommate at the Bürgenstock Resorts, who wanted to get hold of me and had urged Michael to look for me. Tony lives in Calgary and Michael lives in Ottawa.

Easter Sunday 1994 was the usually hectic holiday at the Hyatt Regency in San Antonio. The culinary staff was busy getting ready for the Easter buffet. We anticipated a large crowd. From my office, the lamb roast smelled delicious, and I had promised myself that I would have some for lunch. Suddenly Fernando, one of our servers, peeked through the office window and knocked on the door. "An older gentleman with an attractive young lady out there asked me if he could possibly meet the chef," he said. I promised him I would be out there in a minute. Fernando directed me to a table by the window of our dining room. When I saw who it was, I literarily froze. I recognized him instantly. He was about 80 years old and carried a cane at his side, but he still had the distinct bushy eyebrows and the unmistakable smile on his face. "This cannot be true," I thought. It was Aldo Zarro! He did not recognize me at first; he was not so sure who I was until I mentioned the word "Esplanade." This was a very rare moment. An individual I had admired since I was a young lad was sitting in our restaurant asking to meet the chef! He got up slowly up from his table with the support of his cane, and we hugged each other.

We spent the next two hours drinking champagne and reminiscing about Locarno. Aldo had wanted to meet the chef because he always loved the food at our hotel and felt that there had to be a "Swiss touch" to it. He was right, but never in a lifetime had he expected to see me. What a coincidence. Aldo spent his summers in Acapulco, where he owned a home. On his way to Mexico he always stopped in San Antonio for a few days, where a local bank took care of his assets. We met three more times in San Antonio, while Aldo was in transit from Switzerland to Mexico. In the last letter I received from him in 1998, he expressed his unhappiness with Switzerland's politics and the high taxes and increasing joblessness there. In his last year of his life, my friend found happiness tending to his orchids at his lovely home on Via Nessi in Locarno.

After my son Tony graduated from high school, he spent a year working in Switzerland to build some character. He was very happy to return home, reunite with all of his friends, and start college at South Texas University in San Marcos. Now Tony lives in Austin and works as an IT specialist at the University of Austin and is happily married to Valerie, my Camino *peregrina*, who now teaches English composition at Temple University. My daughter Francesca put herself through school as a waitress, then she worked her way through college at San Marcos. She is now very successful in her career as a speech therapist. She is also happily married to Stephen Slattery. They live here in San Antonio. Greg stayed home with me for a few years, until he decided to marry as well. Now he works as a landscaper at the University of Texas San Antonio and lives with his new wife Antoinette not very far from my home. There are no grandchildren of yet, although I fully qualify to be a grandfather.

I retired at the end of 2010. Our hotel was newly renovated, looking better than ever. Don McDaniel, our general manager, had guided all of us through that experience, and his expertise and experience had made the process easier. In November of that year, the new Q Restaurant, which offers a variety of international barbecue dishes, was completed. I was one of the architects of that new concept, and I knew it was the perfect time to end my professional career and leave the scene. I remembered Don from my time in Dallas, when he was working for Woodbine Development, the owners of the Hyatt Regency in Dallas. Don had always kept a watchful eye on our financial performance. Over lunch at a local restaurant, I told Don of my plans to quit at the end of the year. He had a quick and simple answer: "Eddie, I will follow shortly after you." Don retired in February of 2011. Now, preparation began for an entirely different and new adventure: walking 500 miles on the Camino de Santiago.

Postscript

My son Tony and I traveled to Zurich together in mid-February 2011 to visit some of the places where I had worked in my early twenties. It had been 44 years since I had visited any of those towns. We settled in at my sister's house and started our tour the next day. Engelberg still has its charm, although new hotels and numerous new vacation homes and condos have changed the landscape somewhat. Our first stop, of course, was the old Bellevue Hotel. As we drove by the establishment while we were looking for a parking space, we were able to peek through the window of the room at the south end of the hotel that was my first room away from home. The window still has iron bars on it. The space is now a storage room for ski equipment. Although it was too early for dinner, we entered the hotel's only restaurant, the Yucatan. Nothing had changed very much there. The interior still had the same look and feels it had over 45 years ago. The long wooden bar was the same, as was the service area behind the counter. The big old Stammtisch at the end of the bar was gone, but otherwise it felt just the same.

We seated ourselves at the bar and enjoyed a mug of cold local brew, served by very friendly and attractive female bartenders. They told us that it was Happy Hour and that the beers cost only 2.50 Swiss francs, rather inexpensive for today's prices. We ordered a second round and asked the servers to bring us a menu, eager to learn what kind of food a place named Yucatan was offering. Although both of us were hungry, we agreed not to eat there. Its offerings were an uninteresting variety of tacos, fajitas, and strange-sounding Asian hors d'oeuvres. Since we had just flown in from San Antonio a few days earlier, we weren't interested in trying Mexican food in the middle of the Swiss Alps.

We decided to take a walk up the village. Memories came to life when we passed the sporting goods store and I thought of Teddy's new Volvo on that cold and snowy New Year's Day morning. Where could he be today? I know that I would still recognize him. I was eager to find the old Bierlialp again, our favorite hangout.

We found it, but it had a different name. Now it is a very nice eatery called Restaurant Aubergine. A peek into the restaurant through its large glass windows increased our appetites, and we decided to have some dinner. We ordered a glass of Shiraz and a bottle of sparkling water. The place had a small salad bar that included antipasti items. It featured a wood-fired pizza oven, and its menu offered a variety of entrées featuring veal, lamb, beef, and fresh seafood. We smelled something very good as we watched the few chefs grilling meat over an open wood-fired grill. We both ordered the seared ahi tuna. We watched the chef/owner, Volker Christmann, cut, season, and sear our tuna in his open show kitchen. It was a wonderful meal. We introduced ourselves to Chef Volker and thanked him for the excellent tuna. He was very appreciative and proudly showed us the tuna loin from which he had cut our generous steaks. He told me a bit about his career; he had come through the European Ramada chain. I was impressed with his commitment to high-quality products. After dinner we returned to our home base in Lucerne, delighted that we had skipped the Mexican food at the Bellevue.

Next on our tour was a trip to St. Moritz and Davos. The weather began to clear as we drove our Audi to the southeastern part of Switzerland. Hungry as usual, we stopped at a fifties diner somewhere off the highway for breakfast. We ordered cheese and ham toast with fried eggs and a bowl of Birchermuesli. After a very mediocre lunch at a Savognin Hotel, we arrived at our destination in Bivio, a very small ski resort at the foot of the Julier Pass about 15 miles away from St. Moritz. We did not want to spend $280 to $350 for a room in St. Moritz: the accommodations at Bivio's Solaria Hotel were half the price and very comfortable. After we checked in we tested the car by driving over the Julier Pass. A short time later we arrived in Silvaplana and began the search for the Suvretta House. It had been many years, but well-marked roads guided us to the destination, and it was easy to find the majestic old building. We parked near the hotel and walked around the outside. I wanted to find the area where Chef Mathis looked through the windows at night and identified all of us juice violators. It looked all very familiar, but I was not able to spot the old *garde manger* kitchen through the window. Office space was all I could discover. I couldn't find the old employee entrance. That made sense. Kitchen space is getting smaller today, and I concluded that the good old *garde manger*, where our friend from Basel had jumped into the icy water of the trout tank for 25 Swiss francs, had been replaced by administrative space.

We entered the five-star hotel through its main entrance and were quickly greeted by a *chasseur* who was eager to help us with our ski jackets. We found the lobby bar and were seated at a small round table across from the grand piano. Well trained and very polite waiters quickly appeared to help us. We ordered a carafe of Pinot Grigio. Before the wine was served, a nice linen tablecloth was spread over the wooden table, and a waiter with a small trolley arrived with the glasses and a three-tiered silver stand of bar snacks consisting of beautiful Cerignola olives, Marcona almonds, breadsticks, spiced fresh Melba toast, and some pretzels. The small carafe of Pinot Grigio was served in a silver wine bucket with ice by two different waiters.

Tony and I enjoyed some conversation as we watched the immaculate uniformed waiters tend to guests; they were very quiet and very professional. Suvretta House is still a world-class hotel at its best. The bill for the three deciliters of Pinot Grigio was 62 Swiss francs. The price came as no surprise; I expected it. We left the bar and entered the front desk area, where the *chasseur* was already waiting for us with our jackets; of course he was waiting for a gratuity as well. Many thoughts went through my mind that afternoon at the Suvretta.

Revisting the Suvretta in 2010

We drove downhill from Champfer to St. Moritz and parked our car. It started to get darker and the temperatures fell under the freezing point as we did our sightseeing, and of course we were hungry again. I spotted one of the old hangouts from yesteryear, the Hotel Steffani, now a third-generation-run family hotel. The bar was still there, and the restaurant looked like it had been renovated. My mind traveled back to the sixties, when we had Stavros Niarchos occupying an entire floor at the Suvretta. He used to house all of his private pilots at the Steffani Hotel, all of them on standby around the clock in case Niarchos had to fly somewhere from the nearby Samedan Airport. We settled at the Lapin Bleu restaurant and ordered very traditional and simple Swiss fare; Tony had Kalbsgeschnetzeltes (thin sliced veal with fresh mushrooms and cream sauce) and of course a nicely done *rösti*. I ordered a good old Wiener schnitzel with fries and drank some Calanda Brau. Great, friendly, and efficient service was provided by a predominantly Italian staff. The food tasted great and was simply presented. We walked to get our car from the parking garage to drive back to Bivio, knowing we had to traverse the Julier Pass once more. It was chilly and the increasing snow flurries forced me to drive more slowly; I was no longer accustomed to such weather conditions. We arrived at our hotel and retired for the night.

At the small inn we stayed at in Bivio, Tony and I looked forward to the coffee in the morning. It was always made fresh to order with frothed milk, and it tasted great. The bountiful breakfast buffet included several jams and jellies, some nice cold cuts, excellent cheeses, fruit juice, cereal, and the superb fresh-baked breads you always get in Switzerland. The obligatory Birchermuesli looked very appealing. After we checked out, we drove back to Tiefenkastel and uphill again to Davos. Our first stop was at the Hotel Fluela. I thought it looked better today than it had when I worked there many years ago. We entered the lobby and asked about the restaurant. "It's open," the concierge told us. We ordered our first beer. The Stübli still looked the same, nicely decorated in typical Bündner style. I immediately remembered my quiche story and of course Chef Schmidt with his sauce fetish and his silly peppermill. Our very friendly waitress Fabiola spoke immaculate German and told us that she had grown up in Germany, works in the winters in Switzerland, and lives during the summer in her native country of Spain, near Pamplona.

The elderly gentleman making the rounds in the small restaurant, greeting its customers, was undoubtedly Mr. Hans Gredig, the general manager at the Bürgenstock Hotels in 1966, the one who had chewed my ass out for watching soccer matches on television in the kitchen. Fabiola told me, "Sir, he looked twice at you, like he remembered you from somewhere." Perhaps he did. We left the Fluela and drove to the Belvedere, today a Steigenberger Hotel and still the largest hotel in Davos. After taking a few pictures we returned to the Fluela for lunch. We chose the menu of the day, which featured St. Pierre fish and some Lavaux from Lake Geneva. There was not much activity in Davos; it seemed kind of quiet. The annual World Economic Forum had ended a couple of weeks earlier. My memories from the resort revolved around the two hotels where I had worked during the short time I spent there.

That should have finished our trip to that region of Switzerland, but my son had a different idea; he wanted to visit the principality of Liechtenstein and its capital, Vaduz. A very good suggestion, I thought, since I had never been there either. We were impressed with Vaduz, a clean small city. You can taste the wealth of Liechtenstein, whose citizens enjoy the second-highest per capita income in the world. After having some coffee in a local restaurant, we made our way back to Lucerne for a few days of rest before returning to the United States. During the drive back to my sister's house, my mind started to drift to the Pyrenees Mountains, to the small village of Saint-Jean-Pied-de-Port in France, a place I would travel to in three months to undertake a journey that I still was not able to fully imagine.

Retirement after a long and high-pressure career has its problems. Most everyone will be confronted with this fact sooner or later.

Walking the 500-mile journey had changed my outlook on life. It took me away from the superficiality of the hotel and restaurant business. We really learned to appreciate the simple food we were served during and after endless walks. It brought simplicity back into our lives, an attribute of the increasing popularity of the Camino de Santiago. However skeptical one may be about this pilgrimage and the legendary history surrounding it, it will have an impact on everyone. The simple life and reconnection with nature made Francesca, Valerie, and I conscious of deeper realities. It does not matter if one walks "The Way" for religious, spiritual, cultural, or any other reasons. The day you arrive at the Cathedral Plaza in Santiago de Compostela is impressive and emotional for believers and nonbelievers alike, an overwhelming moment you will never forget.

The "Compostela", now hanging at a wall in my home in San Antonio, serves as a constant reminder of that tranquility and happiness I experienced during the long journey on the Camino.

Recipes

The following recipes refer to places I had worked as a chef and recalling some of the simple and delicious meals we were eating while walking the Camino de Santiago.

Alpen Magronen

8–10 servings

Dr. Odermatt frequently visited the kitchen at the Bellevue Hotel to ask for Alpen Magronen, his favorite dish. We usually had his pasta ready within twenty minutes. Adolf then had plenty time before dinner to have a drink or two and gather with local friends "am Stammtisch," where his wife Ruth, who was already plenty hydrated, was waiting for him.

- 4 medium onions, peeled and sliced
- 2 tbsp. olive oil
- 5 cups milk
- 2 cups heavy cream
- Salt, pepper, and nutmeg to taste
- 1 lb. penne pasta
- 6 cups peeled potatoes, cut into 1-inch cubes

- 16 oz. shredded Swiss or Gruyere cheese
- 4 oz. sweet unsalted butter

Put onions in a nonstick skillet with olive oil. Add a little salt. Caramelize the onions: stir frequently over medium heat until onions are dark brown and soft. This process can take up to 40 minutes—be patient! Halfway through the process of caramelizing the onions, put the milk and heavy cream in a large saucepan and add some salt, pepper, and nutmeg. Bring slowly to a boil. Add the penne pasta and diced potatoes and simmer for 12 to 15 minutes, stirring frequently Take off the heat and set aside when the potatoes and penne are cooked through. Add shredded cheese and sweet butter and incorporate thoroughly. Let the Magronen (penne pasta) rest for awhile and then taste it for flavor and adjust as you see fit. At this time your caramelized onions will be ready also.

Serve on plates and top each serving generously with caramelized onions.

Apple Stew

4–6 servings

You need to serve Alpen Magronen with this fine apple compote. The cheesy and extremely heavy pasta dish makes a delicious combination with sweet apples.

- 3 medium Fuji apples
- 2 tbsp. sweet unsalted butter
- 1 tbsp. dry white wine
- 1/2 lemon juice
- 1 tsp. lemon zest
- 1/2 cup sugar
- 1/2 tsp. ground cinnamon
- Cinnamon stick for garnish

Peel and core apples and cut in eight wedges. Melt butter in a saucepan and add the apple wedges, white wine, lemon juice, lemon zest, sugar, and cinnamon. Simmer over medium heat for

15 minutes, stirring frequently. If the apples are not juicy, add 1/2 tbsp. additional white wine or water, since some apples are juicier than others. Serve warm or cold in a side dish and garnish with a stick of cinnamon.

Pork and Cabbage Stew

8–10 servings

This very simple comfort food is embedded in my memory forever; it was the first hot meal I ate after walking off my job and making my dangerous solo journey on foot over the Surenen Pass, scaring my family, my co-workers, and my bosses to death. Pork and cabbage stew is a specialty of Central Switzerland.

- 1/4 cup canola oil
- 1 1/2 lb. of lean pork shoulder, cut into 1-inch cubes
- 2 small onions, peeled and coarsely chopped
- 1 1/2 heads of green cabbage, cut into 1-inch squares
- 4 cloves garlic, peeled and minced
- 2 cups beef stock or water
- 4 medium carrots, peeled and cut into 1-inch pieces
- 1 cup Riesling wine
- Salt and pepper and some nutmeg to taste
- 1 lb. potatoes, peeled and cut into quarters

Preheat the canola oil in a 5-quart Dutch oven to high heat. Season the pork cubes with salt and pepper. Brown the meat thoroughly and evenly. Add the onions, cabbage, carrots, and garlic. Stir well and add the beef stock or water. Cover Dutch oven with lid and continue cooking over medium heat, stirring occasionally. Taste for flavor and add salt and pepper. Simmer for 1 1/2 hours or until pork is very tender. Remove stew from the heat and add Riesling wine.

Boil potatoes in lightly salted water and serve on the side with the stew.

Minestrone

10–12 servings

Every time I eat a bowl of minestrone, I remember the intern in Locarno, the one we could not stand. I also remember how devilish we were as we made him climb a steep hill behind the hotel to reach that rusty pipe and fill six buckets with dirty water for the soup of the day.

- 3 tbsp. virgin olive oil
- 1 cup celery, diced
- 1 cup onions, peeled and coarsely diced
- 2 cups green or Napa cabbage, cut into squares
- 4 cloves garlic, peeled and coarsely chopped
- 1/2 cup zucchini, diced
- 2 cups fresh green beans, cut into 1-inch pieces
- 1/2 cup carrots, peeled and diced
- 1 cup tomato paste
- 2 1/2 quarts vegetable stock, chicken stock, or water
- 2 cups cooked borlotti or cannellini beans

- 2 cups tomatoes, peeled and coarsely chunked
- 4 cups fresh baby spinach
- 2 cups orzo or any other pasta
- 1/2 cup pesto Genovese
- Salt and pepper to taste

Preheat the olive oil in a large soup pot and add the celery, onions, cabbage, garlic, zucchini, green beans, and carrots. Sauté the vegetables over medium to high heat until they are halfway cooked. Add tomato paste and continue to stir for 2 to 3 more minutes. Add stock or water and the precooked borlotti or cannellini beans, season to taste with salt and pepper, then simmer for 1 1/2 to 2 hours. Add tomatoes, baby spinach, and orzo or other pasta. (If you choose to use spaghetti, break it into small pieces before adding to the soup.) Simmer for another 15 minutes. Turn the heat down to low and add 1/2 cup pesto Genovese for extra flavor.

Serve minestrone with grated Parmesan cheese on the side.

Pesto Genovese

Pesto can be refrigerated for several days. I suggest that you make it a day or two before the minestrone.

- 2 cups fresh basil
- 1 cup flat leaf Italian or regular parsley
- 2 tbsp. pine nuts, lightly toasted
- 4 cloves fresh garlic, peeled
- 1/2 to 3/4 cup virgin olive oil
- Salt and pepper to taste

Put all the ingredients except the olive oil in a food processor. Pulse the ingredients. Add thin streams of olive oil until the pesto looks and feels like a paste. Season with salt and pepper Place pesto in a small container or cup, cover, and store in the refrigerator.

Risotto con Funghi

6–8 servings

This is an Italian dish to eat when you're falling in love. I courted Ermelinda with this dish until Chef Molinari caught me sneaking it out of the kitchen.

- 6 cups chicken stock
- 1 pinch of powdered saffron or one thread of saffron
- 2 cups of sliced mushrooms of your choice (porcini, regular, or portobello mushrooms)
- 1/2 cup chopped onions
- 6 tbsp. sweet unsalted butter
- 1 tbsp. virgin olive oil
- 2 cups Arborio rice or Riso Vialone

- 1/4 cup dry white wine, such as Pinot Grigio
- 1/2 cup grated cheese (Parmesan, Grana Padano, Sbrinz, or Pecorino)
- Salt and pepper to taste

Warm the chicken stock in a saucepan and add a pinch of saffron. In a small skillet, sauté the mushrooms with one tablespoon butter and 1/4 cup of the chopped onions for 3 to 4 minutes. Transfer the mushrooms to a plate or bowl with all of the juices and set aside. Put the olive oil and 1 tablespoon of fresh butter in a sautoir large enough to hold the rice as it expands. (A good measurement tool is to first add the uncooked amount of rice to the sautoir. The rice should not exceed 1/3 the size of the sautoir.) Sauté the rest of chopped onions for one minute, then add the rice.

Add half the prepared chicken stock to the rice and stir constantly over medium heat until the rice starts to absorb the liquid. Add the remaining stock and keep on stirring. After approximately 12 minutes, add the mushrooms and the mushroom liquid to the risotto. Stir over low heat for 1 or 2 more minutes. Check to see if the rice is al dente. If it is, take the risotto off the heat and set aside. It will be perfect by the time you serve it. Then comes my favorite steps: Add the Pinot Grigio, the grated cheese, and the remaining soft butter. Stir and serve at once.

Birchermuesli

6–8 servings

Dr. Bircher believed strongly in what he called the food of sunlight. Around 1900, he suggested that cereals, fruits, and vegetables were more nutritious foods than meat. At that time, meat was regarded as the best food for humans. He created a recipe that is known today as Birchermuesli. It available in stores in just about every corner of the world. Here is my version of the dish.

- 1 cup granola
- 1 cup uncooked oatmeal (quick oats are fine)
- 1 cup plain yogurt
- 1 1/2 cups skim milk

- 1/2 cup honey
- 3 medium apples, cored
- 2 bananas
- 6 to 8 fresh ripe strawberries
- 1 cup grapes
- 1/2 cup fresh blackberries
- 1/2 cup fresh blueberries
- 1/2 cup fresh raspberries
- 1 lemon for juice and zest
- Sprigs of fresh mint for garnish

Mix the granola, oatmeal, yogurt, and skim milk in a stainless steel bowl. Add the honey. With a hand grater, shred the apples, including the peels, into the mixture. Slice the bananas and cut the strawberries in halves or quarters; add the bananas and the strawberries to the muesli. Slowly fold in the grapes and the other fresh berries. Zest and juice the lemon. Sprinkle lemon juice and zest into the muesli.

Refrigerate for at least 15 minutes before serving. Garnish with fresh mint.

Feel free to use different fresh fruit in season, such as mangoes, peaches, and plums. But unpeeled and shredded apples constitute the core ingredient in the muesli. Don't leave the apples out.

Fresh Peach Salad with Raspberries

Makes 6 cocktails

This always was the most popular starter during the warm summer days at the pool restaurant at the Grand Hotel in Bürgenstock. Nobody could peel fresh peaches better than Bruna, our lovely Italian kitchen helper. We were always in the weeds when she had a day off; no one else at the hotel ever developed her skill of removing the skin from five to six cases of peaches in one day! To make it simple, use ripe nectarines.

- Simple syrup (recipe below)
- 1 pint fresh raspberries
- 4 medium ripe peaches
- 3–4 tsp. granulated sugar
- 1/4 cup champagne or dry white wine
- Fresh mint and berries for garnish

Simple Syrup (prepare several hours ahead of time)
- 1 cup granulated sugar
- 1 cup water

Bring sugar and water to a boil and boil until sugar is well dissolved. Chill.

Raspberry Coulis
Place a pint of fresh raspberries into your blender or food processor, add some of the simple syrup to sweeten, and blend. Strain through a sieve. Chill for at least 1/2 hour in the refrigerator. To peel the peaches, have a large bowl ready with enough ice water to cover all the peaches. Then bring enough water to cover all of the peaches to a boil in a saucepan. With a small paring knife, make a small cross incision on each peach. With a slotted spoon, put the peaches in the boiling water for no longer than 20 seconds. Remove the peaches with the slotted spoon and chill immediately in ice water. When the peaches are chilled, carefully remove the skin.

Assembling the Salad
Slice the peeled peaches into small wedges and sprinkle with granulated sugar. Toss carefully and let the fruit stand for a couple of minutes. Put the peach slices into champagne flutes, then spoon some raspberry coulis evenly over the cocktails. Drizzle with champagne or white wine. Garnish with fresh raspberries and mint.

Fegatini in Brodo

4–5 servings

This is the soup that our Italian friend at the Grand Hotel overindulged in week after week. The soup was his first course, followed by *zampone* and lentils for the entrée. We prepared this soup for him every day of his vacation, unless he fell ill and ordered oatmeal.

- 6 oz. chicken livers
- 5 oz. egg noodles
- 1 quart chicken stock
- 5 oz. green peas
- Salt, pepper, and some nutmeg to taste
- 1 tbsp. scallions or chives, thinly sliced

Wash the chicken livers thoroughly in cold water and cut them into quarter-inch cubes. Put livers in a sieve and dip them into boiling water for 30 to 45 seconds to blanch them. Rinse them thoroughly with cold water.

Cook the egg noodles in lightly salted water. Put the chicken broth in a 3- or 4-quart saucepan. Add the noodles, the chicken livers, and the green peas to the chicken stock. Simmer for 3 to 4 minutes and season to taste with salt, pepper, and nutmeg.

Serve *brodo* in large soup cups. Garnish with fresh scallions.

Serve with thin slices of grilled Italian bread and grated Parmesan cheese.

Onion Soup with Gruyere Cheese

6 Servings

- 2 oz. fresh sweet butter
- 2 tbsp. virgin olive oil
- 4 large onions, peeled and sliced thin
- 1 1/2 quarts beef stock
- 12 slices French bread, sliced 1/8 inch thick
- 1/4 cup white wine
- 2 cups grated Gruyere cheese
- Salt, freshly ground pepper, and fresh grated nutmeg to taste

Melt the butter and olive oil in a large soup pot or Dutch oven. Add the sliced onions and some salt and pepper. Slowly roast the onions until they are soft and light brown, stirring frequently. Add the beef stock and simmer for 10 or 12 minutes.

Meanwhile, toast the French bread slices in a toaster or a dry cast-iron skillet until lightly colored.

Just before serving, add 1/4 cup white wine and a dash of nutmeg to the onion soup. Ladle the soup into fireproof glazed pottery bowls. Lay toasted French bread on top of each serving and sprinkle generously with grated Gruyere cheese. Put the bowls of soup topped with bread and cheese on a jelly roll pan and place under the broiler until the cheese bubbles. Serve with a pair of scissors. If the cheese is not manageable, they will add some fun to the meal!

Gazpacho

8–10 Servings

I've carried this recipe with me for over 40 years, and it's still the best and most refreshing gazpacho I've ever tasted. Chef Rüegsegger shared the recipe with me after a Spanish food promotion at the Bürgenstock Resorts.

- 1/2 large onion, peeled
- 3 medium fresh tomatoes
- 1 large yellow bell pepper
- 1 large red bell pepper
- 2 peeled cucumbers
- 4 to 5 garlic cloves
- 1 cup canned red pimientos
- 1 1/2 quarts of vegetable or chicken stock
- 1 cup mayonnaise
- Diced cucumbers, tomatoes, scallions, and bell peppers for garnish
- Thinly sliced toasted French bread

Several hours before serving time, chill serving cups or soup dishes in the refrigerator.

Chunk the onions and tomatoes in 1-inch pieces. Cut the peppers in half, remove the stems and seeds, then cut into 1-inch pieces. Peel the cucumbers and cut them into 1-inch chunks, including the seeds. Place all into a stainless bowl and add the garlic cloves and pimientos.

Pour enough stock over the vegetables to just cover them. Marinate for at least 4 hours in refrigerator. (Overnight is even better.) Puree the stock and vegetables in a blender. Blend in the mayonnaise. Serve the gazpacho in the chilled cups or soup dishes. Garnish with diced cucumbers, tomatoes, scallions, and bell peppers and serve with thin slices of dry toasted French bread.

Italian Salsa Verde

This salsa was one of the condiments we used at the Grand Hotel to enhance our *bollito misto.*, together with fruit *mostarda* and olive tapenade.

- 4 cups of fresh baby spinach
- 4 to 5 anchovy filets
- 1 tbsp. chopped capers
- 2 tbsp. chopped parsley
- 2 garlic cloves, crushed
- Juice of half a lemon
- 1/2 cup virgin olive oil
- Salt and freshly ground pepper to taste

Quickly blanch the baby spinach in boiling water, rinse with cold water, and drain and squeeze well to eliminate all water. Chop the blanched spinach with the anchovies and capers. Add the parsley, crushed garlic, lemon juice, and olive oil. Season with salt and pepper to taste and chill.

Mostarda Cremonese

We never made *mostarda* at Bürgenstock. This delicious fusion of candied fruit and mustard essence is made in Italy and is prepared with whole, chopped, or even pureed fruit. *Mostarda* makes a delicious condiment for fowl, game, beef, and pork and anything in between. These two recipes are my homemade versions. One is made with a variety of dried fruit, ground mustard seeds, and vinegar. The second version is made with fresh seasonal fruit.

Recipe with Dried Fruit
- 1 cup Turbinado sugar
- 1/2 cup white vinegar
- 2 1/2 cups water
- 4 tbsp. powdered English mustard (Coleman's, for example)
- 1/2 cup dried apricots, cut into 1/2 inch cubes
- 1/2 cup dried papaya spears, cut into 1/2 inch cubes
- 1/2 cup dried Greek figs, cut into 1/2 inch cubes

- 1/2 cup dried pineapple chunks, cut into 1/2 inch cubes
- 1/2 cup dried cantaloupe, cut into 1/2 inch cubes
- 1/2 cup dried pears, cut into 1/2 inch cubes
- 2 tbsp. fresh grated ginger

In a saucepan mix the raw sugar with the vinegar and simmer for 5 minutes until the sugar is dissolved. In a small bowl, mix the water with the powdered mustard and add to the sugar and vinegar mixture. Add all of the dried fruit and the grated ginger to the mixture in the saucepan. Simmer over low heat for 40 to 45 minutes. Add more water if necessary. Place into Mason jars and chill overnight before using. This Mostarda will keep for two months.

Recipe with Fresh Fruit
- 8 oz. fresh pears
- 7 oz. fresh quinces
- 9 oz. fresh figs
- 7 oz. fresh peaches
- 7 oz. fresh apricots
- 8 oz. fresh oranges or tangerines
- 2 cups white vinegar
- 4 tbsp. ground mustard seeds
- 1 quart of water
- 4 cups granulated sugar
- 1 tbsp. grated fresh ginger

Peel and core the pears and quinces and cut in quarters. Wash and dry fresh figs; leave them whole. Cut the peaches with skin on into quarters and remove the pits. Cut the apricots with skin on in half and remove the pits. Cut the oranges or tangerines into quarters with the rind on (or slices if you wish).

Heat the vinegar in a small saucepan and add the ground mustard seeds. Stir and set aside to cool. Heat the water in a 3-quart saucepan and add sugar and ginger. Simmer for a few minutes as you would to make sugar syrup.

Add the quinces first and simmer for 20 minutes. Then add the pears. Six or seven minutes later add the apricots. In 6- or 7-minute intervals, add peaches, then the oranges, and finally the figs. Stir gently from time to time.

When all of the fruit has been added, simmer over low heat for another 12 minutes. Take the fruit off the burner and set aside. Allow to cool.

When everything is cooled down, use a slotted spoon and carefully remove the fruit and place in Mason jars.

Mix the vinegar and mustard mixture with the syrup you used to poach the fruit. Pour or spoon slowly into the jars over your poached fruit. Refrigerate. This Mostarda keeps for one month.

Olive Tapenade

6 servings

This is always a great snack when serving hors d'oeuvres or Spanish *tapas*, or you could use it as a spread with fresh-baked breads.

- 1 cup pitted green olives
- 1/cup pitted Kalamata olives
- 1 tsp. capers
- 3 to 4 anchovy filets
- 1/3 cup white onions, cut into chunks
- 1 medium fresh and ripe tomato
- 2 to 3 garlic cloves
- Salt and freshly ground pepper to taste (optional)
- 1/2 cup virgin olive oil

Put all of the ingredients except the olive oil in a food processor and chop them to the consistency you desire. You can chop the ingredients by hand on a cutting board. Place the mixture into a bowl, add some salt and pepper if necessary, then slowly add the virgin olive oil. In most cases, olives and anchovies are salty enough and you may not need additional salt for your Tapenade.

Mix well, cover, and refrigerate. Serve with thin slices of toasted French bread, toasted pita or your favorite cracker

Truite au Bleu (Poached Trout)

1 serving

The day Skinny jumped into that ice-cold trout tank at the Suvretta House in St. Moritz we had to act very quickly to avoid being caught by Chef Mathis. A dozen or so trout flew out of that tank when Skinny landed in it. We had our challenge to retrieve those slippery fish from the floor and return them quickly to their environment.

- 1 small onion
- 1 small carrot
- 1/2 stalk celery
- 2 quarts water
- Salt to taste
- 2 bay leaves
- 1/4 cup vinegar
- 2 sprigs fresh dill(one for the stock and one for garnishing the trout)
- 1 tbsp. peppercorns
- 1 10- to 12-oz. fresh trout, gutted
- 2 small potatoes
- 1/2 lemon juice (for the melted butter)
- 1/2 lemon (for garnishing the trout)
- 2 oz. fresh sweet butter

Prepare a stock: Slice the onion, carrot, and celery into small chunks. Put these vegetables in a 2-quart saucepot with the water, some salt, the bay leaves, the vinegar, the fresh dill and the peppercorns. Simmer for 10 minutes. Drizzle the trout with some vinegar(it will give the trout a bluish color) and carefully place the fish in the simmering stock for 6 to 8 minutes. Serve on a plate with nicely shaped or quartered peeled boiled potatoes, fresh lemon, and a sprig of dill. Drizzle generously with the melted butter and lemon juice.

Sliced Veal "Zurich Style"

1 serving

This is one of the best-known Swiss specialties. You can find it on the menu in most restaurants in Switzerland, and it is served with *rösti*, Switzerland's best-known potato dish. Veal is expensive and isn't available everywhere. You could substitute lean turkey breast, chicken breast, or pork.

- 1 tbsp. virgin olive oil
- 1 tbsp. sweet butter
- Salt, pepper, and paprika to taste
- 7 oz of lean skinless chicken breast, cut in thin strips
- 1/4 cup chopped shallots or onions
- 1 clove garlic, chopped

- 3/4 cup heavy cream
- 1 cup sliced mushrooms (regular, chanterelle, or porcini mushrooms or a mixture)
- 1/4 cup dry white wine
- 1/2 tbsp. fresh lemon juice

Preheat a plate and keep it warm while you're sautéing the meat and vegetables.

Preheat a nonstick skillet and add the olive oil and butter. Season the veal (or whatever meat you're using) with salt, pepper, and some paprika. Put the seasoned meat in a skillet and sauté over high heat until lightly browned. Add the shallots or onions and the garlic and continue to stir until the onions are translucent. Remove the meat, the shallots and onions, and the garlic to the plate you've preheated.

Deglaze the skillet with the white wine. (Deglazing is a process where you add a liquid to the skillet with the residues left from sautéing.) Add the heavy cream and sliced mushrooms. Reduce the sauce over medium heat for two to three minutes. Season this sauce to your taste. Put the sautéed meat with all its juices, the onions and the garlic back into the reduced sauce. Toss and drizzle with lemon juice. Serve with *rösti* potatoes.

Rösti

1 serving

For best results when making a *rösti*, boil the potatoes in their skins one day in advance and chill the potatoes overnight in your refrigerator. Originally, Swiss *rösti* was cooked in pork fat. This recipe offers a lighter and somewhat healthier version.

- 1 large or 2 medium potatoes, unpeeled
- 1/4 cup chopped onions
- 1 tbsp. virgin olive oil
- 1/2 ounce sweet butter
- Salt and pepper to taste

Boil the potatoes in lightly salted water for 35 to 40 minutes, drain the water off, and chill the potatoes overnight in your refrigerator. Peel and grate the potatoes with a box grater or hash brown shredder. In a bowl, mix the chopped onions with the shredded potatoes and season with salt and pepper. Preheat the olive oil and butter to high heat in a nonstick skillet and add the potatoes, mixed with onions. With a turner, form this mixture into a neat patty, but don't press it too hard. Reduce the heat to medium and brown the *rösti* for 4 to 6 minutes. Place a dinner plate upside down over the skillet. Now with the skillet in one hand and the plate in the other hand, flip the *rösti* over onto the plate with its brown side now looking up. Carefully slide the *rösti* back into the skillet to brown the other side until golden. Caution: do this maneuver over the sink in case you have a mishap.

Fresh Guacamole

4–6 servings

This was Patricia's snack each night during her breaks at the Matterhorn Club in Houston. I know she must have liked it; she married me one year later.

- 6 large ripe avocados, peeled and pitted
- 1 jalapeno pepper or 2 Serrano chiles, cut in half and seeds removed
- 1/4 cup chopped onions
- 1 diced fresh tomato
- 2 tbsp. chopped cilantro
- 1 fresh lime, for juice
- 1 fresh orange, for juice

Put the avocados in a bowl and then add all of the other ingredients, including the lime and orange juice. Season with salt and freshly ground pepper to taste. Use a kitchen whisk to bring the avocado mixture to the chunkiness you desire.

Serve well chilled with corn tortilla chips and your favorite salsa.

Flan (Crème Caramel)

This simple custard dessert is popular everywhere. Custard is used in countless desserts, such as crème brûlée, Crème Catalane, open-faced fruit pies, charlottes, or savory quiche, to name a few. The flan with caramelized sugar is popular just about anywhere and was featured on most menus during our pilgrimage in Spain. My two *peregrinas* sometimes ordered flan on midmorning breaks as they were walking the Camino.

8 servings

- 3/4 cup sugar, divided
- 2 cups heavy cream
- 3 eggs
- 1 tsp. vanilla extract
- 1 tsp. lemon zest
- 1/4 cup sugar
- 1 pint of fresh raspberries
- Fresh mint for garnish

Put 1/2 cup of the sugar in a small heavy skillet. Stir continuously with a wooden spoon over medium heat until the sugar starts to caramelize. The sugar is caramelized when it turns the color of a caramel candy. It becomes a caramel-colored liquid. The brown liquid stage is somewhere near 335° Fahrenheit. Spoon the caramelized sugar carefully into the bottom of eight 5-ounce ramekins.

Heat the cream in a small saucepan almost to the boiling point, then remove from heat.

While you are making the custard for the flan, preheat the oven to 300° Fahrenheit.

Make the custard: In a stainless steel bowl beat the eggs thoroughly. Add the vanilla extract, the lemon zest, and the remaining 1/4 cup of sugar. Add the heated heavy cream, stirring with a whisk to incorporate. Ladle this mixture into the ramekins and put the filled ramekins in a 9 x 12 inch baking pan. Fill the pan with warm water until the level of the water is about 3/4 of the height of ramekins.

Bake for 45 to 50 minutes. Check occasionally with a thin needle or a knife with a sharp point to determine if the flan is ready. If the needle or knife comes out clean, the flan is done. Put the flans in your refrigerator and chill at least two hours before serving. Garnish the finished desserts with raspberries and fresh mint.

Grilled Strip Sirloin with Chimichurri

The Gallego food festival in Logroño was a great break after 100 miles of walking. We were in a celebratory mood; we had never walked 100 miles in our lives! The festival was very reminiscent of a Texas backyard barbecue. I was hungry and eager to taste everything they had to offer, from *pulpo* to grilled sausages, ribs, chicken, and a big juicy piece of sirloin with a spicy herb crust. It reminded me of the *chimichurri*-marinated sirloins we offered on the new menu at the renovated Q Restaurant at the Hyatt Regency in San Antonio.

4 servings
- 1 thick cut, 2 lb. strip sirloin steak or rib eye,
- Salt and cracked peppercorns to taste
- 1 cup *chimichurri* marinade (recipe below)
- *Chimichurri salsa roja* (recipe below)

Season the sirloin or rib eye with salt and cracked peppercorns and coat generously with *chimichurri* marinade. Allow the beef to sit for two to three hours in the marinade. Grill or broil the sirloin to your desired temperature. Carve the beef for individual servings. Serve with *chimichurri salsa roja*.

Chimichurri Marinade

- 1/2 cup virgin olive oil
- 1/2 cup sherry vinegar
- 1/4 cup water
- 2 cups chopped parsley
- 4 fresh scallions
- 3 to 4 cloves garlic, crushed
- 1 pinch cayenne pepper
- 1 tsp. salt
- 1/2 lemon or lime juice
- Fresh ground pepper to taste
- A hint of dried oregano

Combine and mix all ingredients in a blender.

Chimichurri Salsa Roja
8 to 10 servings

- 1/2 tsp. whole cumin seeds
- 1/2 cup chopped parsley
- 1 tsp. dried oregano
- 4 cloves garlic, peeled
- 2 cups canned pimentos, well drained
- 3 tbsp. Spanish paprika
- 1/2 cup Spanish sherry vinegar
- 3 cups virgin olive oil
- Sea salt, freshly ground pepper, and ground cumin seeds

Place the whole cumin seeds, the chopped parsley, the dried oregano, the garlic cloves, the pimentos, the paprika, the sherry vinegar, and the olive oil into a food processor or blender and puree to the thickness you desire.

Season with salt, pepper, and ground cumin.

Gravlaks (Scandinavian-style cured salmon)

Try this at home while you freeze a bottle of Aquavit. It is the Scandinavian version of smoked salmon with champagne. I learned about gravlaks when I was living in Minnesota. It was the best-selling lunch item at the Minneapolis Rosewood Room, where we served it with a shot of Aquavit.

- 1 side of boneless salmon filet with skin on
- 1 oz. salt per pound of salmon
- 1 oz. granulated sugar per pound of salmon
- 1/2 tbsp. cracked peppercorns per pound of salmon
- 1 tsp. cracked juniper berries per pound of salmon
- 1 cup fresh chopped dill per pound of salmon
- 1 to 2 cups canola oil
- Sweet Dill Sauce (recipe below)

Carefully remove all of the remaining bones from the salmon filet. With a sharp knife, punch several holes into the skin.

In a bowl, mix salt, sugar, cracked peppercorns, and cracked juniper berries. Rub these ingredients into the salmon on both sides. Then coat both sides with chopped dill. Put the salmon filet in a shallow pan and drizzle with canola oil. Cover with another shallow pan with some weight on it to slightly press the salmon. You may use two 20-oz. tomato cans to add weight. Keep the gravlaks in the refrigerator for at least 48 hours to allow it to cure.

Slice gravlaks like smoked salmon at a 45-degree angle. Serve with small boiled potatoes in their skins, sweet dill sauce, and fresh lemon.

Sweet Dill Sauce
- 2 cups mayonnaise
- 1/4 cup Dijon mustard
- 2 tbsp. sugar
- 1/3 cup fresh chopped dill leaves
- Juice of 1/2 lemon

Mix all ingredients and chill.

Egg Foo Young

6–8 servings

These small Chinese omelets were the cause of panic at a late-night banquet at the San Francisco Hilton when the whole batch of 250 egg foo youngs flipped over in our rotating oven and burned beyond recognition. We were lucky it didn't happen on the next course, which was Peking duck!

- 6 eggs
- 1/2 cup chopped onions
- 1 cup of fresh bean sprouts
- 1/4 cup sliced fresh scallions
- 6 oz. fresh peeled shrimp, cut in small chunks
- 1/2 tsp. sesame oil
- 2 tbsp. light soy sauce
- 1/4 tsp. corn starch

Beat the eggs well in a stainless steel bowl. Sauté the onions, bean sprouts, scallions, and shrimp in sesame oil in a frying pan over high heat. Dust with the corn starch and add soy sauce. Add all these ingredients to the beaten eggs. With a 2-ounce ladle, spoon this mixture onto a hot griddle or into a hot frying pan and cook the omelets quickly on both sides.

Basque Piperade

8–10 Servings

A delicious pepper sauce that is used in both French and Spanish Basque cuisine. It is also used for egg dishes like omelets. It is kind of like a Basque ranchero sauce. This *piperade* tasted delicious with the breaded and fried pig feet I ate in St.-Jean-Pied-de-Port the day before we started to cross the Pyrenees.

- 3 tbsp. virgin olive oil
- 1 green bell pepper, seeded and chopped
- 1 red bell pepper, seeded and chopped
- 2 Anaheim peppers, seeded and chopped
- 4 cloves garlic, peeled
- 1 cup chopped onions
- 1 tbsp. Spanish paprika
- Pinch of sugar
- 4 medium fresh tomatoes, chopped
- 1 cup diced canned tomatoes with its juice
- Salt and freshly ground pepper to taste

In a large skillet, heat the olive oil and sauté the peppers, garlic, and onions with the paprika until the vegetables are slightly soft. Season with salt and a pinch of sugar.

Now add fresh and canned tomatoes to the *piperade*. Simmer for 10 minutes, until some of the liquid evaporates. You can increase the heat of the *piperade* by adding two or three chopped Serrano peppers.

Chipirones with Caramelized Onions

4 servings

I saw this dish a dozen times when I was walking the trail. The night before we returned home to Texas, I finally tried it in a neighborhood restaurant in Madrid.

- 3 large onions
- 1/2 cup virgin olive oil, divided in half
- 10 medium-size squid bodies (the cleaned main body of the squid without the tentacles)
- 10 squid tentacles
- Salt and freshly ground pepper to taste

Peel and slice the onions and put in a frying pan with half of the olive oil. Sauté the onions for 30 to 40 minutes over medium heat, stirring frequently until the onions appear soft and turn light brown.

Now grill the squid: Wash the squid bodies and tentacles and carefully pat dry with paper towels. Put the squid on a plate and season generously with freshly ground pepper and some salt. Drizzle olive oil over the squid. Grill the bodies and tentacles over very high heat for 3 to 4 minutes on each side, preferably in a cast-iron skillet. Remove from heat.

On each serving plate, lay the squid body on a generous amount of caramelized onions. Put the grilled tentacles beside each grilled squid body. Drizzle virgin olive oil over the squid and serve with Fresh Sautéed Spinach and Roasted Pine Nuts (recipe below).

Sautéed Spinach with Toasted Pine Nuts

- 8 cups fresh baby spinach
- Virgin olive oil
- Salt and pepper
- 2 tbsp. lightly dry-roasted pine nuts

Sauté the baby spinach with a drizzle of virgin olive oil and season with salt and pepper. Mix with the pine nuts. Serve with Chipirones.

Pimientos de Padrón

2 servings

This is a classic in any *tapas* bar and lots of fun to share with your friends, especially when you find out who gets the hot chili. Don't forget the beer. The small whole green chiles originate and are named after the city of Padrón in Galicia.

- 15 to 20 whole Padrón peppers
- 1 tbsp. sea salt
- 2 tbsp virgin olive oil

Sprinkle some sea salt over the chilies and drizzle with olive oil. Quickly roast the Padrón peppers in a very hot cast-iron skillet. Serve in a bowl.

Roasted Pimento Vinaigrette

After a long day of walking on the hot Spanish plains, Christof and I ordered a huge bowl of salad at a restaurant in Fromísta. The greens were tossed with sensational pimento vinaigrette. I tried to reproduce the recipe at home and nailed it.

- 1/3 cup blanched almonds
- 1/2 cup onions, cut in chunks
- 2 cloves garlic, peeled
- 1/2 cup canned pimentos, well drained
- 1 tbsp. sweet paprika
- 1tbsp. Dijon mustard
- Juice of 1/2 lemon
- Juice of 1/2 orange
- 1 tbsp chopped parsley or cilantro
- 1/3 cup Spanish sherry vinegar

- 1 cup virgin olive oil
- Salt and pepper to taste

Toast the almonds lightly in a skillet. As soon the almonds show some color, take them off the heat at once and let them cool. Put the almonds and all the ingredients except the olive oil and the salt and pepper into a blender. Blend thoroughly to a smooth texture. Slowly add the olive oil and blend for another minute. Season with some salt and freshly ground pepper.

Transfer the dressing to a bowl, cover, and refrigerate. This dressing makes also a delicious dip for crudités, artichokes, and asparagus.

Papas Bravas

4 servings

This *papas* helped me regain my energy after a long walk into the city of Pamplona.

- 4 large potatoes
- 1/4 cup chopped onions
- 4 cloves garlic, chopped
- 1tbsp. virgin olive oil (for the Brava sauce)
- 1 1/2 cups virgin olive oil (for frying the potatoes)
- 1 tbsp. sweet paprika
- 1 tbsp. Tabasco or Cholula sauce
- 3/4 cup ketchup
- 3/4 cup mayonnaise

Peel the potatoes and cut them into cubes or strips. Fry the potatoes in a skillet in 1 1/2 cups hot olive oil. Drain the potatoes and put them in a bowl. Sprinkle with some salt and pepper.

Make the Brava Sauce: In a skillet, sauté the chopped onions and garlic with 1 tablespoon of olive oil until soft. Remove from heat and add the paprika and the Tabasco or Cholula sauce. Add the ketchup and mayonnaise and whisk gently to incorporate. Season to taste with salt and pepper.

Drizzle the Brava Sauce generously over the seasoned fried potatoes and serve.

Grilled Lamb with eggplant, papas and tomatoes

4 servings

This dinner in Triacastela was very welcome after we crossed O Cebreiro and then walked for 30 kilometers through a rainy Galicia.

- 8 lamb chops, 4 oz. each (two chops for each serving)
- 1/2 cup virgin olive oil
- 2 lemons
- 2 each medium size tomatoes
- 1 each medium eggplant
- 4 each medium sized potatoes
- Salt and pepper to taste

Season the lamb chops with salt and freshly ground pepper and rub with some of the olive oil. Grill the chops in a hot cast-iron skillet or pan-fry the lamb chops over high heat to your favorite temperature. Lamb should preferably be a nice pink color on the inside and should have a medium to firm touch to it.

Gambas al Ajillo (Prawns in Garlic)

4 servings

This is another of my favorite *tapas* dishes. It is simple and always delicious and is very quick and easy to prepare. Some Spaniards insist that the shrimp should not be peeled because it increases the flavor of the dish. I agree.

- 1/2 cup virgin olive oil
- 4-5 peeled garlic cloves, cut into small slices
- 1 bay leaf
- 1 pinch red pepper flakes
- 1 tsp. Spanish paprika
- Juice of 1 lemon
- 2 oz. dry Spanish Sherry

- 1 lb. fresh shrimp, unshelled
- 1 fresh baked French baguette

Use a heavy frying pan or a cast-iron skillet. Preheat the olive oil and add the garlic slices, the bay leaf, and the pinch of red pepper flakes. Stir over low to medium heat until the garlic is lightly browned. Add the Spanish paprika, the lemon juice, the sherry and all of the shrimp.

Turn up the heat and simmer for approximately 3 minutes. Take off the heat. Let the shrimp rest for 10 minutes, and then transfer the *gambas* with all of the juices to a shallow platter. Serve with sliced baguette for delicious dipping.

Vieras a la Gallega (Scallops Galician Style)

4 servings

After many weeks of eating *bocadillos* and simple *peregrino* meals while walking the Camino trail, we could not get enough of this Galician scallop dish at Barolo's Seafood Restaurant in Santiago de Compostela. It is presented in a scallop shell, the symbol of the Camino de Santiago. All along the route, scallop shells guide pilgrims on their journey. *Vieras* can be served as an appetizer or as an entrée. Serve it with any dry white wine, or even better with a Spanish Albariño.

- 1 tbsp. virgin olive oil plus oil for drizzling
- 1/4 cup chopped onions
- 1 tsp. chopped garlic

- 1/2 cup canned plum tomatoes, diced and drained
- 1 tsp. sweet paprika
- 1 tbsp. canned pimentos, diced
- 1 tbsp. bread crumbs
- 4 medium prawns, shells removed
- 4 medium to large scallops, shells reserved
- Salt and freshly ground pepper to taste
- 1/2 lemon for garnish
- 2 cups rock salt or kosher salt

Sauce

Preheat the tablespoon of olive oil in a nonstick skillet. Sauté the chopped onions and chopped garlic until they are soft. Add the tomatoes, the paprika, and the pimentos and cook on low heat for 2 or 3 minutes. If the sauce seems too thin, add a tiny bit of the breadcrumbs to firm it up. Season with salt and pepper to taste. Put the sauce in a cup and set aside.

Season the prawns and scallops with salt and freshly ground pepper and drizzle with olive oil. Preheat a cast-iron skillet and sear the prawns and scallops for 1 minute on each side, turning frequently to prevent burning. Remove the seafood from the skillet and set aside.

Spoon some sauce into each scallop shell and put one prawn and one scallop on top of the sauce. Put some more sauce over the seafood and sprinkle each serving with some bread crumbs. Drizzle with olive oil and place the shells in a shallow baking pan.

Place the pan under a broiler until the bread crumbs are slightly browned. Put half a cup of rock salt on each plate to prevent the shells from sliding. Put one shell on each plate and garnish with fresh lemon.

Spanish Olive Bread with Pesto

Makes one loaf of bread

The crazy restaurant owner in Villafranca del Bierzo who promoted his famous steaks from that 3,000-pound bull served a delicious roll with some olives in it. When I returned home to Texas, I tried it and added some pesto to the recipe. It turned out perfect.

- 18 oz. flour
- 1/2 oz. dry yeast
- 1/4 oz. salt
- 1 1/4 cup warm water
- 3/4 oz. pitted Kalamata olives, coarsely chopped
- 3/4 oz. pitted green olives, coarsely chopped
- 1/2 oz. pesto (see recipe above)

Put the flour, yeast, and salt in a mixing bowl. Add the water and mix on low speed for 5 minutes. Add the chopped olives and the pesto. Mix on low for 5 more minutes. Change to medium speed and mix for 1 minute.

Let the dough rise for 2 hours at room temperature. Punch the risen dough down and let it rest for another 30 minutes.

Roll the dough into the shape of a bread loaf. Dust with some flour if necessary to prevent the dough from sticking to your rolling pin and bread board.

Put the dough in a baking pan lightly sprayed with olive oil. Let the dough rest for 15 more minutes. While the dough is resting, preheat the oven to 400° Fahrenheit. Put the baking pan in the oven and bake for 25 to 30 minutes. Let the bread cool for at least half an hour before serving.

Tortilla Espagnole (Spanish Tortilla)

2 servings

We ate this almost every day as we walked the Camino de Santiago. It's a great snack any time of the day. It's Camino food that will give you energy!

- 1 1/2 cup of thinly sliced raw potatoes
- 1/2 cup virgin olive oil
- Salt and freshly ground pepper to taste
- 1/2 medium size onion, coarsely chopped
- 4 large or 5 medium eggs

Wash the potatoes, but do not peel them. Cut the potatoes lengthwise in half and cut into slices 1/8 inch thick.

Preheat half of the olive oil in a nonstick skillet. Add the sliced raw potatoes and the salt and pepper and slow roast the potatoes over medium heat until they are soft but not overcooked. Stir frequently to make sure the potatoes do not turn brown or crisp. Add the onions and sauté for 2 or 3 more minutes. Put this mixture into a medium-size bowl, including the olive oil you cooked the potatoes with. Set the bowl aside and let everything cool for 5 minutes.

In another bowl, whisk the eggs thoroughly, then pour them over the potatoes and onions and stir to mix the ingredients.

In the same skillet, preheat the remaining olive oil. Over low to medium heat cook the egg, potato, and onion mixture just like you would cook scrambled eggs.

After 4 or 5 minutes, place a large dinner plate upside down over the skillet. With the skillet in one hand and the plate in the other hand, flip the tortilla onto the plate with its brown side looking up, just as you would do for *rösti* potatoes. Slide the tortilla back into the skillet brown t side up. Continue cooking the tortilla without stirring until the bottom side is browned. Serve on a large plate with freshly baked French bread. Tastes great with some *piperade*.

Zarzuela de Mariscos (Spanish Crustacean Stew)

8 servings

Zarzuela de Mariscos is the Spanish version of bouillabaisse.

Base Stock
- 1/3 cup virgin olive oil
- 1 fresh yellow Bell pepper, cut into 1/2 inch squares
- 2 fresh Anaheim peppers, cut into rings and seeds removed
- 1 cup peeled and diced carrots
- 1 cup coarsely chopped onions
- 1 bunch of scallions, cut into 1 inch lengths
- 4 cloves garlic, chopped
- 2 bay leaves
- 3 tbsp. tomato paste
- Thread of saffron

- 1 piece of lemon peel
- 2 tbsp. sweet paprika
- 2 cups water
- 1 28-oz. can plum tomatoes
- 1 lb fresh mussels (Prince Edward Sound)
- 12 littleneck clams
- 6 calamari tubes cut into rings
- 6 calamari tentacles
- 12 large shrimp, unshelled
- 12 large scallops
- 1 cup white wine
- 2 fresh tomatoes, peeled, seeds removed, and cut into 1-inch chunks
- 2 tbsp. coarsely chopped Italian parsley
- French bread, thinly sliced and toasted
- Garlic-infused olive oil
- Salt and freshly ground pepper to taste

Preheat the olive oil in a large Dutch oven. Add the peppers and diced carrots and sauté for 3 to 4 minutes over medium heat.

Now add the chopped onion, sliced scallions, garlic cloves, bay leaves, tomato paste, saffron thread, lemon peel, and paprika. Sauté all the ingredients over low to medium heat for approximately 3 to 5 minutes, stirring constantly. Add the water and the plum tomatoes with all their juice. Season this stock to taste with salt and pepper. Simmer this soup base for 30 minutes over low heat.

Add mussels and clams to the broth and simmer until the shells open. Then add the calamari rings and tentacles, the shrimp, and the scallops. Bring everything to a simmer, then remove from heat and let the *zarzuela* rest for 5 minutes. Add the white wine.

Serve in individual soup bowls. Garnish each serving with a few chunks of the fresh tomatoes and sprinkle with coarsely chopped parsley. Serve with thinly sliced toasted French bread that has been dipped in garlic-infused olive oil. A bottle of chilled, crisp Albariño is a must to accompany this fine shellfish stew.

Banana Soufflé

2 servings

This is a very simple and refreshing dessert. No soufflé pump required!

- 2 teaspoons butter, softened to room temperature
- 1 to 2 tbsp. granulated sugar (if the banana is very ripe, use only 1 tbsp.)
- 1 ripe banana, peeled
- 2 egg whites
- Fruit sorbet

Butter the bottom and sides of two 5-oz. soufflé ramekins. Add a teaspoon of granulated sugar to each cup. Tilt the ramekins and turn them in your hands until bottom and sides are covered with sugar. Put ramekins in the refrigerator.

Preheat oven to 350° Fahrenheit.

In a stainless steel bowl, thoroughly mash the banana with a fork. In another bowl rigorously beat the egg whites with a whisk to a firm peak. Add the rest of the granulated sugar and whip for one more minute to incorporate the sugar. With a rubber spatula carefully fold the beaten egg whites into the well-pureed bananas. Do not whip, just fold.

Put the prepared ramekins in a flat baking pan. Carefully spoon the soufflé batter into the ramekins all the way to the rim. Bake for 12 to 14 minutes, until the soufflés rise one inch above the top of the ramekins. Serve with a scoop of your favorite sorbet.